~~TREATISE~~

OF

SMALL ARMS, FIELD PIECES,

𝕰𝖙𝖈.,

FOR THE USE OF

HER MAJESTY'S SHIPS.

The Naval & Military Press Ltd

Published by the
The Naval & Military Press
in association with the Royal Armouries

Unit 10 Ridgewood Industrial Park,
Uckfield, East Sussex, TN22 5QE
Tel: +44 (0) 1825 749494
Fax: +44 (0) 1825 765701

MILITARY HISTORY AT YOUR FINGERTIPS
www.naval-military-press.com

ONLINE GENEALOGY RESEARCH
www.military-genealogy.com

ONLINE MILITARY CARTOGRAPHY
www.militarymaproom.com

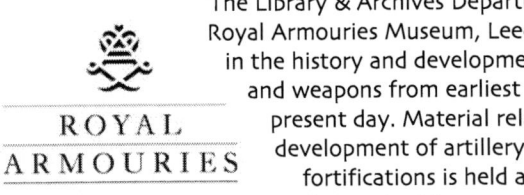

The Library & Archives Department at the Royal Armouries Museum, Leeds, specialises in the history and development of armour and weapons from earliest times to the present day. Material relating to the development of artillery and modern fortifications is held at the Royal Armouries Museum, Fort Nelson.

For further information contact:
Royal Armouries Museum, Library, Armouries Drive,
Leeds, West Yorkshire LS10 1LT
Royal Armouries, Library, Fort Nelson, Down End Road, Fareham PO17 6AN

Or visit the Museum's website at
www.armouries.org.uk

In reprinting in facsimile from the original, any imperfections are inevitably reproduced and the quality may fall short of modern type and cartographic standards.

Printed and bound by CPI Antony Rowe, Eastbourne

CONTENTS.

	PAGE
Organization of Seamen for Landing	1
Instruction for Landing Seamen, Marines, and Field Pieces	3
List of Stores and Ammunition for Boats going on Service	6

RIFLE EXERCISE.

Memorandum on Carrying the Rifle	10
Orders for Company Drill	11

THE MANUAL EXERCISE .. 14

Piling Arms	19
Slinging Arms	20
On moving Men with Arms "Shouldered" or "Ordered"	21

THE PLATOON EXERCISE .. 22

To Load and Fire Standing	22
,, Kneeling	26
Remarks on Loading and Firing	30
Orders for a Battalion or Column to Load	31
Independent or File Firing	32
Exercise to Receive Cavalry	33

FORMATION OF A COMPANY .. 35

Officers' Places	35
To Form Four Deep	36
Inspecting a Company	37
Dismissing a Company	38
Movements of a Company	39
To form a Rallying Square	44

FIELD EXERCISE FOR A BATTALION OF SEAMEN .. 46

Officers' Places	46
Manœuvres	48
To Form a Square Four Deep	53

CONTENTS.

	PAGE
LIGHT INFANTRY MOVEMENTS	54
Skirmishing	59
Advance Guard	64
Patrols	66
Rear Guard	66
EXTRACTS FROM THE INSTRUCTION OF MUSKETRY FOR THE ARMY	67
Target Drill	70
Target Practice	71
DIRECTIONS FOR PRESERVING AND CLEANING ENFIELD RIFLES	72

CUTLASS EXERCISE.

Explanation of the Target	76
Preparatory Movements	77
The Training Cutting Exercise	79
The Training Guarding Exercise	83
The Training Pointing Exercise	86
The Training Combination Exercise	90
Class Practice	93
Inspection Exercise.	94
THE ATTACK AND DEFENCE	96
The Engaging Guard	97
First Practice—Cutting and Guarding	98
The Rallying Practice	99
Second Practice—Pointing and Guarding	100
Third Practice—The Combination	104
Tabular arrangement of the Practices	106
Concluding Observations, and Rules for Loose Play	107
BAYONET OR PIKE EXERCISE	109
PISTOL EXERCISE	112
FIELD PIECE EXERCISE	116
Ranges for 12-pr. and 24-pr. Howitzers	124
FIELD BATTERY DRILL	126
Preliminary Observations	126
Telling Off and Proving	127
Posts of Officers	128
Manœuvres	129
SCALING LADDER EXERCISE	134
ARTICLE ON FIELD FORTIFICATION	136

INSTRUCTIONS

FOR THE

EXERCISE OF SMALL ARMS, FIELD PIECES, &c.

FOR THE USE OF

HER MAJESTY'S SHIPS.

ORGANIZATION OF SEAMEN FOR LANDING.

As the efficiency of Seamen when landed in any considerable number, depends most materially upon a proper system of organization and training previous to their being landed, and without which they are inefficient, the following system is to be strictly observed in all Her Majesty's Ships:—

1st.—The Small-arm men are to be formed into Companies of 80 men, with 3 Petty Officers, each Company to be commanded by a Lieutenant, with 2 Mates, or Midshipmen.

2nd.—Every Ship of the Line is to have two Companies properly drilled and trained for landing, Frigates one Company, and Sloops half a Company.

3rd.—The Men to be armed with Rifles and Bayonets, each Company is to be told off into Subdivisions and Sections, and to be exercised in such movements as are absolutely necessary to manœuvre a Company, by the Officers who are appointed to command them.

4th.—The Companies when landed are to fall in and number from the right, according to the seniority of the Captains of their respective Ships, Flag Ships being No. 1 and 2, so that they at once will fall into their places according to their numbers when landed: each Ship of the Line is to be prepared to land with their Small-arm men, 6 Pioneers, viz., 2 with a Saw and Axe each, 2 with a Pickaxe and Spade each, 2 with a small Crowbar and Sledgehammer; Frigates will send 3, and Sloops 1, the tools to be slung on the Men's backs.

5th.—When landed for service, each man is to have 60 rounds of ammunition, each Ship is to send a Bugler with her men if she has one; he is to be able to sound the "Assembly," the "Retreat," "Commence Firing," "Cease Firing," "Close," and "Extend," which sounds the Men are to be accustomed to on board.

6th.—If the Men are likely to be on shore during the night, they should have a haversack and blanket slung across their shoulders.

7th.—As muskets are apt to miss fire the first time, if not properly clean, the greatest precaution is to be taken to see that the nipple is perfectly clear before loading; first, by blowing down the barrel and placing the finger to feel if the air passes through the nipple, and afterwards by snapping a cap off to dry up any oil or moisture that may be in the barrel.

8th.—When Field Pieces are landed, the guns are to be brigaded together according to their calibre, numbering from the right in the same manner as a Company.

9th.—Line-of-Battle Ships should send an Armourer with cleaning rods, screw drivers, spare nipples, &c.

10th.—When firing in close order the front rank should fire *kneeling*, as owing to the shortness of muskets accidents are frequently taking place.

Scale of Companies to be sent from each Ship.

Line-of-Battle Ships, 2 Companies of 80 Men each.
Frigates .. .. .. 1 ,, ,, ,,
Sloops .. .. .. ½ ,, ,, ,,
10 Companies to form a Battalion.

INSTRUCTIONS

FOR LANDING SEAMEN, MARINES, AND FIELD PIECES.

For Exercise or Service on Shore.

1. THE boats should be formed in divisions according to the seniority of the Captains of their respective Ships, numbering from No. 1 on the right. The Seamen and Marines should be told off in Companies previous to leaving their ships, and on landing they will form immediately in the same order.

The Field Howitzers should be mounted as Boats' Guns, the Field Carriages and Limbers being stowed in the bottom of the boat. The crew should be told off to their respective duties for landing Gun and Limber, 9 men being stationed to the Gun and the remainder to the Limber. On the boat touching the beach, the Gun Nos. should immediately jump out, mount the carriage, and run it up to the bows to receive the Gun, which should be hoisted out by small sheers, or by a tackle hooked to a strop half way up the mast; but in the case of surf, the Gun should be thrown overboard, and hauled on shore by a hawser or drag-ropes. The Limber and Limber-boxes should be passed out by hand; when landed, the Gun is to be limbered up, or brought at once into action, according to circumstances.

2. Each division of boats should have a distinguishing flag. Launches will carry two scaling-ladders, intrenching tools, &c.; barges and pinnaces, one ladder each.

3. The boats will always land a boat's-length apart. Before leaving the ships, four boat-keepers for each gunboat, and two for the others, with an Officer in charge of each division of boats, are to be told off, and are on no account to leave them.

A fast-pulling boat with Medical Officers will attend in rear of the line.

4. Should the distance from the point of landing be considerable, the boats of each division, in tow of each other, commencing with the lightest boats, will pull in,—the leading boat of each division abreast, leaving space for the whole to form line abreast when ordered; on approaching the beach, the tow-ropes should be cast off, and the gunboats dress up in line, ready to open fire if necessary to clear the beach. The Officer in command will commence firing from the gunboats when he thinks fit, but no musketry is to be fired without orders.

5. When the Commanding Officer perceives the beach to be cleared (or when he considers it proper), he will order "Cease Firing," and direct the boats with Skirmishers and light Field Pieces to pull in and land as quickly as possible. On landing, they will immediately extend, but not open fire till the Officer commanding them sounds "Commence Firing." The Main body then pull steadily in and land, forming line in rear of the Covering party. The Field Pieces form on the flanks of their own Divisions, or in Batteries, according to orders. The scaling ladders remain in rear until required for service. The Main body being formed, they will advance in line or column according to circumstances, preceded by the Skirmishers, firing if necessary.

6. After landing, the boats should be hauled off into deep water to prevent a surprise, and those with guns might be employed on the flanks, to cover the advance or retreat when practicable.

7. Should the boats be employed for the disembarkation of troops, the same arrangement as to the divisions of boats should remain. It will then be desirable that every boat should carry a flag similar to that of the Commanding Officer of its Division,

and when in large numbers the boats should also be painted according to the colours of the flags, that the troops may readily know their own boats.

On these occasions the launches, barges, and pinnaces will form a front line so as to clear the beach, the light boats will tow troop, paddle-box boats, &c., and be ready to succour any boats that may be damaged by the enemy's fire.

8. The re-embarkation should be conducted on similar principles to the disembarkation; the Skirmishers and Light Field Guns extending in rear of the line, which will then "pass by fours from the right of Companies to the rear," through the intervals, forming line again if necessary to support the Skirmishers, who will retire firing, and re-form in rear of the line; they are again extended, and so on until the Main body have embarked. The Covering party then embark under cover of the boats' guns.

N.B.—The following Boatswain's Calls will be found useful amongst Seamen in the event of there being no Bugler.

"Extend," .... "Pipe down or Veer Cable."
"Close," .... "Stand by Hammocks."
"Commence Firing,".. "Lower."
"Cease Firing," ...... "Belay."
"Assembly," .... "Pipe to dinner."

ON MANNING AND ARMING BOATS.

THE following is a list of Stores that are required for Boats when called away "manned and armed," with the number of Officers and Men required for the undermentioned Boats:—

Launches pulling 20 oars; barges, pinnaces, and paddle-box boats pulling 14 oars; cutters pulling 10 oars, and gigs 4 oars.

Boats' crews to be armed with cutlass and rifle; bowmen, coxswains, carpenters, and gunners with cutlass and pistol.

Nature of Stores, &c.	Launches.	Barges, Pinnaces, PaddleBox.	Cutters.	Gigs.
Crew required in the Boat	21	15	11	4
Gunner's Mates, or Seamen Gunners	2	1	..	..
Carpenter's Crew	1	1	..	..
Marines	14	8	4	2
Nature of Guns	24 P^r H^r	12 P^r H^r	..	..
Priming Wire and Tube Box for each Gun	1	1	..	..
Spare Trigger Line, Vent Bit, and Spare Lock or Hammer	1	1	..	..
Spare Breeching	1	1	..	..
Sponge, Rammer, and Worm	1	1	..	..
Cartridges	48	48	..	..
Round Shot	24	24	..	..
Spherical Case filled	12	12	..	..
Common Shell filled	12	12	..	..
Common Case	6	6	..	..
Wood Fuzes	30	30	..	..
Set of Instruments for fitting Fuzes	1	1	..	..
Tubes for each Gun	80	80	..	..
Range Table	1	1	..	..
Muskets for Blue Jackets	18	12	8	4
Ammunition for each Musket	60	60	60	60
Percussion Caps	2,500	1,500	1,000	500
Revolver Pistols	6	5	3	3
Cartridges for each Pistol	50	50	50	50
Caps for Pistols	400	350	200	200
Pikes	4	4	4	2
Tomahawks	4	4	2	1
Cutlasses	24	17	11	4
Blue Lights	4	2	2	2
Rockets	4	4	2	2
Water Baricoes, full	10—9 gal.	6—9 gal.	6—7 gal.	3—7 gal.
Provision Baricoes	4	2	2	1
No. of days' Provisions, or according to circumstances	2	2	2	2

Carpenter's Bag, containing

Fearnought and grease, nails, set of tools, strips of copper for oars, corks for stopping musket holes, and other materials for stopping leaks.

Boatswain's Bag, containing

Lead and line, cable punches and cold chisels, canvas, palm, needle and twine, rounding, spunyarn, and marlinespike.

Boat's compass, and anchor and cable in each boat; masts and sails, 2 spare oars, spyglass, signal book, ensign and answering pendant; two tourniquets, a saw, axe, and sheet lead, bucket and piggin, lantern and candles, and slow match.

NOTE.—When it is considered desirable, more ammunition than is here laid down should be sent away in each boat, the powder being stowed in half cases.

RIFLE EXERCISE.

MEMORANDUM.

Rifles are at all times, when unloaded, to be used with the cock down on the nipple, and sentries may be permitted to carry their arms when loaded in the same manner, in order to secure the cap in its place; but to avoid accidents, they are to be carried on all other occasions at *half cock* after being loaded.

ORDERS FOR COMPANY DRILL.

"Attention." "Number."
(*Tell off by Subdivisions and Sections.*)
"Tell off 'Right,' 'Left.'"
(*Prove the Company by* "*Shoulder,*"
"*Slope,*" *and* "*Order Arms.*")
"Shoulder Arms."
"To the Right Face."   "Front."
"To the Left Face."   "Front."
"Right about Face."   "Front."
"Left about Face."   "Front."

(*The movements of the feet are not to be taught.*)

"Mark Time."
"To the Right turn."   "Front turn."
"To the Left turn."   "Front turn."
"Right about turn."   "Front turn."
"Left about turn."   "Front turn."
"Halt."   "Dress."
"Right close." "Quick March." "Halt."
"Left close." "Quick March." "Halt."
"Fours deep."   "Front."
"Fours about."   "Front."
"Fours right."   "Front."
"Fours left."   "Front."
"Order Arms."   "Stand at Ease."

INSPECTION OF ARMS.

"Attention." "Shoulder Arms."
"For Inspection, Rear Rank take open order." "March."
"Port Arms."   "Fix Swords."
"Half Cock Arms."   "Examine Arms."
"Ease Springs."   "Return."
"Shoulder Arms."   "Unfix Swords."
"Order Arms."
"Rear rank take close Order." "March."
"Shoulder Arms."

"MANUAL EXERCISE."

"Rear rank take open Order."   "March."
"Secure Arms."   "Order Arms."
"Shoulder Arms."   "Fix Swords."
"Present Arms."   "Shoulder Arms."
"Shoulder Arms."   "Charge Swords."
"Slope Arms."   "Shoulder Arms."
"Stand at Ease."   "Rear rank take close
"Attention."   Order." "March."
"Carry Arms."   "Order Arms."
"Trail Arms."   "Unfix Swords."
"Shoulder Arms."   "Stand at Ease."
"Order Arms."   "Attention."
"Trail Arms."   "Shoulder Arms."

"PLATOON EXERCISE."

(*The Rear Rank close up 9 inches.*)
"As a front and rear rank standing, in slow time."
"Prepare to load."
(*The whole make a* "*Right half face,*" *the front rank then step out with the left foot 10 inches to the left front, and the rear rank 6 inches to the front.*)

"Load."   "Return."
"Rod."   "Cap."
"Home."
"At * * * yards, Ready."
"Present."
(*To be given quickly.*)

(*After firing make a pause, taking the time from the right, come to the* "*capping*" *position, put down the flap, and taking the time from the right, come to the position of* "*prepare to load.*")

"In quick time—Load."

(After loading make a pause, taking the time from the right, come to the "capping" position, and proceed to cap, which must always be done after loading.)

"Shoulder Arms."

(Bring the left foot back to the right, and come to the front. Rear rank always step back as they "shoulder.")

"Fire one round as a company in quick time."

(Rear rank close up.)

"At * * * yards, Ready."

(The whole make a "Right half face," the front rank then step out 10 inches to the left front, and the rear rank 6 inches to the front.)

"Present."

(After firing put down the flap, and come to the position of "prepare to load;" go on with the loading in quick time, then "cap" as before, and wait for orders.)

"Shoulder Arms."

"Fire one round by subdivisions from right to left."

(Rear rank close up.)

"Right Subdn. at * * * yards, Ready."

(Make the "half face," and step out as before.)

"Present."

(After firing put down the flap, "load" and "cap" as before.)

"Left Subdn. at * * * yards, Ready."

(Make the "half face," and step out as before.)

"Present."

(After firing put down the flap, "load" and "cap" as before.)

"Right Subdivision—Shoulder Arms."

"Left Subdivision—Shoulder Arms."

"Company will Fire a Volley and Shoulder."

(Rear rank close up.)

"At * * * yards, Ready."

"Present."

(After firing put down the flap, close the heels, then after a pause, taking the time from the right, come to the "shoulder.")

"Order Arms."

"Company will load from the order."

(Rear rank close up.)

"Load."

(Step out and go on with the loading in quick time, and "cap" as before.)

"Order Arms."

(Rear rank step back.)

"Company will make ready from the order."

(Rear rank close up.)

"At * * * yards, Ready."

"Present."

(After firing put down the flap, "load" and "cap" as before.)

"Shoulder Arms."

"Independent file firing from the right (left or centre) of Company."

(Rear rank close up.)

"Commence."

(They judge their distance, step out and make "Ready" as before.)

"Cease Firing."

(They complete their loading and "shoulder," front and rear rank together.)

"Company will fire a Volley kneeling."

(Rear rank close up.)

"At * * * yards, Ready."

(The whole make the "Right half face," the front rank then carry the right knee 12 inches to the rear and 6 inches to the right, the rear rank 12 inches to the rear and 12 inches to the right.)

"Present."

(After firing put down the flap, "load" and "cap" kneeling.)

"Shoulder Arms."

"Company will fire a Volley and Shoulder."
"Front Rank Kneeling."
(*Rear rank close up.*)
"At * * * yards, Ready."
(*The whole make the "Right half face," the front rank then kneel as before.*)
"Present."
(*After firing put down the flap, make a pause, and "shoulder," front and rear rank together.*)
"Order Arms."
"Company will load from the order."
(*Rear rank close up.*)
"Load."
"Order Arms."
(*Rear rank step back.*)
"Company will extend from the Right, (Left or Centre.)"
"* * * paces from the Right (Left or Centre) Extend."
(*The named file drops on the knee in the "capping" position; the remainder "shoulder arms" as they step off, rear rank men looking out for the distance, and drop on the knee in the "capping" position on attaining their distance.*)

"Commence Firing."
(*They judge their distance, the rear rank continue in the "capping" position, reserving their fire till the front rank has re-loaded and "capped."*)
"Cease Firing."
(*They complete their loading and remain steady.*)
Note.—The inclines may be practised, as they are very useful in skirmishing.
"On the Right (Left or Centre) Close."
(*The whole rise up, "trail arms," and close on the named file.*)
"Stand at Ease."
"Attention."
"Pile Arms."
"Stand Clear."
"Break."
"Fall in."
"Stand to."
"Unpile Arms."
"Shoulder Arms."
(*Then proceed with Company Formations.*)

N.B.—If File marching with *Right* in front, the Company can be formed to the "Front," "Right," or "Right about." If with *Left* in front, to the "Front," "Left," or "Left about."

The Company marching in file has only to "Halt" and "Front," to be formed to the *left* or right flank, according as the *right* or left is in front.

In Countermarching, always do so on the front rank.

In telling off Subdivisions and Sections, the Right Subdivision has the odd file if any, and the Flank Sections have the odd files if any. If obliged to have one Section weaker than the other, it is to be the 3rd. The 1st and 3rd Sections are termed "Right Sections," and the 2nd and 4th, "Left Sections." When there is a blank file, it should always be the *third* from the left.

When using ammunition, the arms and pouches are to be examined after firing.

THE MANUAL EXERCISE.

Note.—The Manual and Platoon Exercises are *first* to be taught in small detachments of not more than 10 men in Single File.

The Rifle to be carried at "Shoulder arms" in the right hand at the full extent of the arm; guard to the front between forefinger and thumb, the remaining fingers under the cock; barrel close into the shoulder.

Manual Exercise.
Rear rank take open order.
(*If two deep.*)

. The right and left hand men of the rear rank step back one pace, and face to their right, to mark the ground on which the rear rank is to halt.

March.

At the word "March" they face to the front, and the rear rank step back one pace dressing by their right.

Secure Arms.

Seize the rifle with the left hand at the lower band, raising it a few inches with the right, and slip the thumb under the cock, fingers under the guard.

"Two."

Carry the rifle to the left side, and grasp it with the left hand as high as the shoulder, the barrel to the front and perpendicular, bringing the right hand at the same time under the cock.

"Three."

Cant the butt with the right hand, under the left arm, then bring the right hand smartly to the right side; the left elbow to be thrown a little to the rear, the guard *just* visible, the thumb on the stock, the fingers grasping the barrel, and the hand rather below the hip.

Note.—In marching when the cap is on, the cock will be brought up under the armpit, the sling resting on the arm; but at other times the rifle may be carried with the barrel downwards, the right hand grasping it above the lower band, the left grasping the right arm below the elbow.

MANUAL EXERCISE. 15

SHOULDER ARMS.
    Bring the rifle to the perpendicular position with the left hand, seizing it at the same time with the right hand under the cock.

"Two."
    Carry the rifle to the right side in the right hand, and hold it with the thumb and forefinger round the guard at full extent of the arm, remaining fingers under the cock, seizing it at the same time with the left hand in line with the elbow, to steady it in the shoulder.

"Three."
    Bring the left hand smartly to the left side.

PRESENT ARMS.
    Seize the rifle with the left hand at the lower band, raising it a few inches with the right, and slip the thumb under the cock, fingers under the guard.

"Two."
    Raise the rifle with the right hand to the *poise*, bringing it in front of the centre of the body, *lock* to the front, left hand smartly on the stock, wrist on the guard, fingers pointing upwards, thumb in line with the mouth, right elbow and butt close to the body.

"Three."
    Bring the rifle down with a quick motion as low as right hand will admit, guard to the front, and grasping it with the left hand just above the lock plate, draw back the right foot so that the hollow of it may touch the left heel. The rifle in this position to be totally supported in the left hand, close in front of the centre of the body.

SHOULDER ARMS.
    Bring the rifle to the right side and seize it with the right hand, the thumb and forefinger round the guard, at full extent of the arm, the remaining fingers under the cock, bringing the left hand square with the left elbow and right foot to the left.

"Two."
    Bring the left hand smartly to the left side.

Slope Arms.	Seize the rifle with the left hand at the lower band, raising it a few inches with the right, and slip the thumb under the cock, fingers under the guard.
"Two."	Bring the rifle to the left side and grasp the butt with the left hand, the right holding the small, the muzzle to slant to the rear, with the guard pressed against the hollow of the shoulder, the elbow close into the side.
"Three."	Bring the right hand smartly to the right side.
Stand at Ease.	Bring the right hand smartly across the body and place it on the left, at the same time move the left foot 6 inches to the front, bending the left knee, and let the weight of the body rest chiefly on the right leg.
Attention.	Bring the left foot back to the right, and the right hand smartly to the right side.
Carry Arms.	Seize the small of the butt with the right hand.
"Two."	Bring the rifle to the right side, and seize it as in "Shoulder Arms," the left hand to be brought across the body to steady it there.
"Three."	Bring the left hand smartly to the left side.
Trail Arms.	Seize the rifle with the left hand in line with the elbow.
"Two."	Bring the rifle to a horizontal position at the right side, seizing it at once with the right hand just behind the back sight, and holding it at full extent of the arm, at the same time bringing the left hand smartly to the left side.

NOTE.—Whenever the word "Trail Arms" is given, every Rear rank man, if at close order, will take a short pace to the rear, so that the muzzle of his rifle may be just in front, and clear of, the wrist of his front rank man.

MANUAL EXERCISE.

SHOULDER ARMS.

"Two."

Bring the rifle to the perpendicular position with the right hand, and seize the trigger-guard between the forefinger and thumb, at full extent of the arm, remaining fingers under the cock; at the same time seizing the rifle with the left hand, in line with the elbow, to steady it in the shoulder.
Bring the left hand smartly to the left side.

ORDER ARMS.

"Two."

Seize the rifle with the left hand in line with the right shoulder.
Bring the rifle down in the left hand as low as the arm will admit; seize the rifle between the bands with the right hand, and place the butt quietly on the ground; bring the left hand at the same time smartly to the left side, the right arm to be slightly bent, and the thumb *in rear* of the barrel.

TRAIL ARMS.

Bring the rifle to the horizontal position at the right side, holding it with the right hand just behind the back sight, at full extent of the arm.

NOTE.—"Change Arms." Bring the rifle to a perpendicular position at the right side, seize it with the left hand close above the sight and carry it round to the left side, bringing it to a horizontal position at the full extent of the arm.

"Trailed arms" for the ease of the men may be used on the line of march, or in marching to or from the place of exercise, or with guards marching to and from their posts, or when moving as light infantry; but they must never be used with fixed bayonets or swords, except in preparing to charge; nor in file marching; nor in any field movements where close marching is required.

ORDER ARMS.

Bring the rifle at once to a perpendicular position at the right side, and place the butt quietly on the ground with the right hand, keeping the arm slightly bent, and the thumb *in rear* of the barrel.

Fix Swords.

Place the rifle with the right hand between the knees, guard to the front, and draw the sword out with the right hand, holding the scabbard with the left; then seize the rifle with the left hand, at the upper brass, and fix the sword with the right, sliding the spring on to the catch and the ring on to the muzzle; afterwards seize the rifle with the right hand between the bands, bringing the left smartly to the left side, and taking the time from the right, come to the position of " Order Arms."

Shoulder Arms.

Raise the rifle with a smart cant of the right hand, and seize the trigger-guard between the forefinger and thumb, at full extent of the arm, remaining fingers under the cock; at the same time seize the rifle with the left hand in line with elbow to steady it in the shoulder,

"Two."

Bring the left hand smartly to the left side.

Charge Swords.

Make a "Right half face" and bring the rifle down nearly to a horizontal position at the right side, muzzle inclining upwards a little, the left hand to grasp the piece firmly at the lower band, the right hand holding the small of the butt; the rear rank to remain at the " Shoulder."

NOTE.—It is to be understood, that whenever a Battalion in line charges with swords, the whole in the first instance are to advance at a firm quick step with "Shouldered arms." At the command "Prepare to Charge," the rifles of the front rank will be brought to the "Long Trail," and those of the rear rank to the Slope. At the word "Charge," the rifles of the front rank will be brought smartly to the charging position, and the pace increased to "Double March," carefully preserving the line, and avoiding too much hurry. The enemy being routed, it will depend on the Officer Commanding to give the word "Halt," when both ranks will "Shoulder arms," and proceed as may afterwards be directed.

Shoulder Arms.

Bring the rifle into the shoulder and steady it as before by the left hand, at the same time facing to the front.

"Two."

Bring the left hand smartly to the left side.

Rear Rank take Close Order. March.

At the word "March," the rear rank closes within one pace.

MANUAL EXERCISE.

ORDER ARMS. { As before.

UNFIX SWORDS. { Place the rifle with the right hand between the knees, guard to the front, and seize it with the left hand at the upper brass, as also the handle of the sword with the right; then press the spring inwards with the forefinger and raise the sword, dropping the point towards the scabbard, at the same time move the left hand to the scabbard to guide the sword into it; this being done, seize the rifle with the right hand, and taking the time from the right, come to the position of "Order Arms."

STAND AT EASE. { Push the muzzle of the rifle to the front with the right hand, arm close to the side, at the same time move the left foot 6 inches to the front.

PILING ARMS.

The Company standing in close order, with "Ordered Arms."

PILE ARMS. { At the word "Pile," the rear rank will take a pace of 10 inches to the rear; at the word "Arms," the front rank will face about, bringing their rifles with them to "Ordered arms."
The front and rear rank men will then place the butts, locks inwards, against the inside of their outer feet, as close to the heel as possible; after which the right file rear rank and the left file front rank will incline their rifles towards each other and cross ramrods; the right file front rank will at once place his left hand round the muzzle of his left file, bearing it from him, and with his right hand lock ramrods by passing his between the ramrods, and to the right of the muzzles of the other rifles; the left file rear rank will then lodge his rifle between the muzzles of the rifles of the front rank, sling uppermost. When there is an odd file the front and rear rank man will lodge his rifle against the pile nearest his right hand.

STAND CLEAR.	Ranks take a pace of 10 inches backwards and face towards the pivot flank.
STAND TO.	Ranks facing towards the pivot flank will face inwards, and close on their arms by taking a pace of 10 inches forward.
UNPILE ARMS.	At the word "Unpile," seize the rifle with the right hand under the top band; at the word "Arms," unlock the ramrods without hurry, by inclining the butts inwards, and come to "Ordered arms;" the front rank will then "front," and the rear rank close on it by taking a pace of 10 inches forward.

NOTE.—It is necessary to be careful in piling and unpiling arms to prevent damage being done to the ramrods and sights.

SLINGING ARMS.

The Company standing in close order with "Shouldered Arms."

SLING.	Raise the rifle a few inches with the right hand, seize the sling with the left, about a foot from the upper band, and place it over the head. Dip the right arm in front between the rifle and the body, and seize the small of the butt inside the sling, then draw the muzzle to the left shoulder with the left hand, the right holding the small of the butt.
SHOULDER ARMS.	Bring the butt with the right hand about a foot to the front, seizing the sling with the left. Dip the right arm in rear between the rifle and the body, and seize the trigger guard between the forefinger and thumb, then lift the sling over the head with the left hand and come to the position of "Shoulder Arms."

NOTE.—The above is made out with a view to slinging arms for going aloft or hauling on ropes, &c., as in this case they must be slung *muzzle up;* for if slung muzzle down, the butt being heaviest will invariably cause the rifle to cant round, and thus much inconvenience the man carrying it. But if working in the water, they must be slung with the *butt up* to keep the lock from getting wet.

Remarks.

The motions in the Manual Exercise are to be performed, having one pause of the slow time of march between each, except that of "Fixing Bayonets" or "Swords," in which a longer time must be given; one pause should also be made between the first and last parts of the words of command—for instance, " Shoulder " (one pause), " Arms," both in the Manual and Platoon.

A Company or Battalion is never to come to the " Halt " or "Form in Line" but with " Carried Arms."

When men are to move in *quick or double time,* it is to be understood, as a general rule, that as they make the first step they " Slope Arms," if at the " Shoulder," without any separate word of command; and on being halted, arms are instantly " Carried " in the same manner.

When moving from the " Halt " with arms "Ordered," it is to be understood, as a general rule, that the men " Trail Arms " without any separate word of command; and at the word " Halt" arms are to be " Ordered," when the rear rank will close to the front.

If required to move a few paces backwards or forwards when at " Ordered Arms," the rifle is merely to be raised from the ground, keeping the barrel close to the shoulder.

THE PLATOON EXERCISE.

To Load and Fire Standing.

PLATOON EXERCISE. — At this caution the Rear rank, if there be two ranks, will take a pace of 9 inches to the front.

As a Front (or Rear) Rank Standing in Slow Time.

PREPARE TO LOAD.

"Two."

From Shouldered Arms.

Seize the rifle with the left hand in line with the shoulder, at the same time make a "Right half face." Carry the left foot 10 inches to the left front as a *front* rank, or 6 inches to the front as a *rear* rank, moving the body with it; at the same time square the shoulders to the front, and bring the rifle down in the left hand, placing the butt quietly on the ground, close against the inside of the left foot, barrel to the front and perpendicular; slip the left hand smartly to the upper brass, carry the right at once to the pouch, and take from it a cartridge.

From Ordered Arms.

Make a "Right half face," carrying the rifle round with the body.

Carry the left foot 10 inches to the left front as a *front* rank, or 6 inches to the front as a *rear* rank, moving the body with it; at the same time square the shoulders to the front, and pass the rifle smartly to the left hand, which will seize it at the upper brass, placing the butt quietly on the ground, close against the inside of the left foot, barrel to the front and perpendicular; carry the right hand at once to the pouch and take from it a cartridge.

PLATOON EXERCISE.

Load.	Bring the cartridge to the forefinger and thumb of left hand and tear off the end with care.
"Two."	Shake the powder into the barrel.
"Three."	Reverse the cartridge, and place the bullet into the barrel nearly as far as the top, holding the paper above it between the forefinger and thumb.
"Four."	Tear off the paper that remains, and seize the head of the ramrod with the forefinger and thumb.
Rod.	Force the ramrod half out and seize it back-handed, the elbow square with the shoulder.
"Two."	Draw it entirely out, turning it at the same time to the front, put it on the top of the bullet, turning the back of the hand to the front.
Home.	Force the bullet down till the second finger of the right hand touches the muzzle.
"Two."	Press the ramrod lightly towards you, and slip the two forefingers and thumb to the point, and grasp it as before.
"Three."	Force the bullet steadily down to the bottom.
"Four."	Ascertain that the bullet is home, by two steady pressures, avoiding all sharp strokes.
Return.	Draw the ramrod half out, catching it back-handed, with the elbow square.
"Two."	Draw it entirely out, turning it to the front; put it into its place, and force it home quickly; then seize the head of the ramrod between the forefinger and thumb, and drop the left hand smartly to its full extent, and seize the rifle.
Cap.	Let the shoulders resume the "half face," and bring the rifle to a horizontal position at the right side, with the left hand grasping it behind the back sight, the right holding the small of the butt, pressing it against the hip as a front rank, or 4 inches above it as a rear rank, and half cock the rifle.
"Two."	Throw off the old cap (after having fired), take a cap from the pocket, put it on the nipple, and press it down with the thumb, then carry the hand to the small of the butt quietly.

PLATOON EXERCISE.

AS A FRONT (or Rear) RANK AT * YARDS. READY.**

From the Capping Position.	From Shouldered Arms.	From Ordered Arms.
Adjust the sight with the forefinger and thumb of the right hand, placing the top of the sliding bar *even* with the line, or to the place that indicates the elevation necessary for the distance named; then raise the flap steadily, if required, after which bring the hand back to the small of the butt, and full cock the rifle, keeping the fingers behind the trigger guard and the eye steadily fixed on some object in front.	Make a "Right half face," at the same time seize the rifle with the left hand in line with the elbow. "*Two.*"—Bring the rifle to a horizontal position at the right side, grasping it with the left hand behind the back sight; the small of the butt as a *front rank*, pressed against the hip—as a *rear rank* 4 inches above it; then carry the left foot 10 inches to the left front as a *front* rank, and 6 inches to the front as a *rear* rank, and proceed as detailed in first column.	Make a "Right half face," carrying the rifle round with the body. "*Two.*"—Bring the rifle to a horizontal position at the right side, grasping it with the left hand behind the back sight, and proceed as explained in the adjoining columns.

PRESENT.

Bring the rifle to the shoulder, pressing the butt firmly into the hollow of it with the left hand, which must grasp the rifle as in the capping position, the right hand holding it at the small, the right elbow slightly raised (but not so much as to impede the aim of the rear rank man); bring the left elbow well under the rifle to form a support, the muzzle inclining to the bottom of the object, at the same time shut the left eye.

"Two."

Raise the muzzle slowly until the fore sight is aligned through the back sight with the object the right eye is fixed upon, at the same time placing the forefinger on the trigger.

"Three."

Pull the trigger with the second joint of the finger by a steady pressure, without the least jerk or motion of the hand or elbow, keeping the eye still fixed on the object.

"Four."

Bring the rifle down to the Capping position, and shut down the flap, then seize the rifle with the right hand close in front of the left, count a pause of the slow time, taking the time from the right, and come to the position of "Prepare to Load."

LOAD. { As before directed.

To Shoulder from the Capping Position.

SHOULDER ARMS.
{ At the word "Shoulder," bring the left foot back to the right, and at the word "Arms" face to the front, at the same time bring the rifle up to the right shoulder with the left hand, the fingers extended and in line with the elbow to steady it, the upper part of the barrel in the hollow of the shoulder, the forefinger and thumb of the right hand placed round the guard, the remaining fingers under the cock.

"Two." Bring the left hand smartly to the left side.

NOTE.—The Rear rank, if there be two ranks, will take a pace of 9 inches to the rear, as they "Shoulder."

To Order from the Capping Position.

ORDER ARMS.
{ At the word "Order," bring the left foot back to the right, and seize the rifle with the right hand close in front of the left; at the word "Arms" face to the front, and with the right hand place the butt quietly on the ground at the right side, coming to the position of "Ordered Arms," as in "Manual Exercise."

NOTE.—The Rear rank will take a pace of 9 inches to the rear as they "Order."

To Load and Fire Kneeling.

From Shouldered Arms.

PLATOON EXERCISE. { At this caution the Rear rank, if there be two ranks, will take a pace of 9 inches to the front.

AS A FRONT (or Rear) RANK KNEELING IN SLOW TIME.

PREPARE TO LOAD. Seize the rifle with the left hand in line with the elbow, at the same time make a "Right half face."

	Front Rank.	*Rear Rank.*
"Two."	Sink down smartly on the right knee, which is to be drawn back 1 foot to the rear, and 6 inches to the right of the left heel, the right foot being perpendicular and under the body, square with the right knee, the left leg to be as upright as possible; bring the rifle down in the left hand close to the body, and pass the butt to the left rear over the right heel to the extent of left arm, sling upwards, meeting the muzzle with the right hand; slip the left hand under the top swivel, and keep the rifle close into the side and as upright as possible, at the same time carry the right hand to the pouch and take from it a cartridge.	Sink down smartly on the right knee, which is to be drawn back 1 foot to the rear and 1 foot to the right of the left heel, the right foot being perpendicular and under the body, square with the right knee, the left leg to be as upright as possible; turn the body nearly to the right, and carry the rifle in the left hand, and place the butt on its flat, lock uppermost, under the shin of the right leg of the front rank man of the file on the right, meeting the muzzle with the right hand; slip the left hand under the top swivel, keeping the muzzle as high as the right shoulder, at the same time carry the right hand to the pouch and take from it a cartridge.

LOAD.	{	As before directed.
ROD.	{	,, ,,
HOME.	{	,, ,,

RETURN.
{ Draw the ramrod half out, catching it back-handed with the elbow square.

"Two."
Draw it entirely out, turning it towards the ground, put it into its place and force it home quickly; then seize the head of the ramrod between the forefinger and thumb, and slip the left hand smartly to its full extent and seize the rifle below the lower band.

CAP.
{ Let the body resume the "Right half face," and bring the rifle to a horizontal position at the right side, the front rank passing the rifle round in front of the left leg; place the left forearm square on the left thigh, and proceed as detailed when "Capping" standing.

PLATOON EXERCISE.

	From the Capping Position.	From Shouldered Arms.	From Ordered Arms.
AS A FRONT (or Rear) RANK AT *** YARDS. READY.	Bring the weight of the body on to the right heel, then adjust the sight, as before explained; after which bring the right hand back to the small of the butt, and full cock the rifle, keeping the fingers behind the trigger guard, and the eye steadfastly fixed on some object in front.	Make a " Right half face," at the same time seize the rifle with the left hand in line with the elbow. " Two."—Drop the rifle to a horizontal position at the right side, grasping it with the left hand behind the back sight; and sink down smartly on the right knee, which is to be drawn back 1 foot to the rear and 6 inches to the right of the left heel as a *front rank*, or 1 foot to the rear and 1 foot to the right of the left heel as a *rear rank*, the right foot being perpendicular and square with the right knee, the left leg straight; bring the weight of the body on to the right heel, the left forearm resting on the left thigh, and proceed as detailed in first column.	Make a " Right half face," carrying the rifle round with the body. " Two."—Bring the rifle to a horizontal position at the right side, grasping it with the left hand behind the back sight, and proceed as explained in the adjoining columns.

NOTE.—When required to come to the "Ready" kneeling from the Capping position standing, the left foot is to be brought back to the right, before sinking down on the right knee.

PLATOON EXERCISE.

PRESENT.

"Two."
"Three."

"Four."

Bring the rifle at once to the "Shoulder," as before directed when standing, without raising the body off the heel, and place the left elbow on the left knee to form a support.

As before drected.

" "

Bring the rifle down to the Capping position, at the same time raise the body off the right heel, and place the left forearm square on the left thigh, then shut down the flap easily, and return the hand to the small of the butt; count a pause of slow time, taking the time from the right, and carry the rifle in the left hand round in front of the left leg as a *front* rank, or turn the rifle over in the left hand as a *rear* rank, coming to the position of "Prepare to load," as before directed.

NOTE.—When required to Load standing from the kneeling position, after shutting down the flap, seize the rifle with the right hand close in front of the left, and rise smartly to the "half face," bringing the right foot to the left, and still keeping the rifle in a horizontal position at the right side; then, after counting a pause, turn the barrel at once downwards, bringing the rifle to a perpendicular position, and proceed as detailed in the *Second* motion of "Prepare to Load" standing.

LOAD. { As before directed.

To Shoulder from the Capping Position.

SHOULDER ARMS.

"Two."

At the word "Shoulder" spring smartly up to the "half face," bringing the right foot to the left, still keeping the rifle in a horizontal position at the right side.

At the word "Arms" face to the front, and bring the rifle up to the "Shoulder," as before directed.

Bring the left hand smartly to the left side.

NOTE.—The Rear rank, if there be two ranks, will take a pace of 9 inches to the rear as they "Shoulder."

PLATOON EXERCISE.

To Order from the Capping Position.

ORDER ARMS.
> At the word "Order" spring smartly up to the "half face," bringing the right foot to the left, still keeping the rifle in a horizontal position at the right side, and at the same time seize the rifle with the right hand close in front of the left.
>
> At the word "Arms" face to the front, and with the right hand place the butt quietly on the ground at the right side, coming to the position of "Order Arms," as in Manual Exercise.

NOTE.—The Rear rank, if there be two ranks, will take a pace of 9 inches to the rear as they "Order."

REMARKS.

The men being thoroughly grounded in the foregoing instructions, may now be practised in two ranks at "close order" in the different firings, as a Company in line, as a Wing of a Battalion firing a volley, File firing, &c.

In firing by Companies, the sliding bar will generally be set to the correct distance before the firing commences, the men will then be required to raise the flap only, and cock the piece at the word "Ready;" but when the squad is exercised in slow time, it will be advisable, for the sake of practice, that some arbitrary distance should be given. Whenever no distance is given, each man must judge for himself the distance from the object he is to aim at.

Too much pains cannot be taken to ensure that the men take a deliberate aim at some specified object whenever they bring the rifle to the "Present," and if no natural object presents itself, several small bull's-eyes must be marked on the ship's side.

In coming to the "Present," the inclination of the right cheek to the butt depends entirely on the distance the men may be directed to fire at, or on the elevation given to the rifle; if at a short distance, it must lay on the butt without too much stooping of the head; but if firing at the longer distances, the head must be raised according as those distances increase; particular care must also be taken that the men in this position shut their left eye when taking aim, looking along the barrel with the right eye, which is to continue fixed on the object after the fire has been given, to ascertain that he has not deranged his rifle from the true alignment by pulling the trigger. The necessity of restraining the breathing when pulling the trigger should also be impressed on the men.

If after repeated firing there should be any difficulty in ramming the ball home, the rifle should be held between the knees, and both hands applied to the ramrod to force the ball home, avoiding all heavy strokes except as a last resource.

In firing in two ranks, either standing or kneeling, great care is necessary with the short rifles that the rear rank men are sufficiently close to fire *clear* of the front rank men.

When a Column or Line is required to Load, the Command is to be

WITH CARTRIDGE. { At this caution the rear rank will take a pace of 9 inches to the front.

LOAD. { The loading to proceed in the quick time, but taking the time from the right in coming to the Capping position. When in column, or when any person is immediately in front, the rifle, when brought to the Capping position, is to be *slanted upwards*, in order to prevent the possibility of an accident.

CEASE FIRING. { At the command, "Cease Firing," the Company, having completed its loading and capped, will receive the order "Shoulder Arms;" but if at the "Ready" when the "Cease Firing" sounds, it will be ordered to "Half Cock Arms," as follows.

HALF COCK ARMS. Place the thumb on the cock and the forefinger on the trigger, and draw both back till the cock is free, then ease it gently down close to the nipple, removing the forefinger from the trigger, and draw it back to the "half cock;" after which put down the flap, and carry the right hand to the small of the butt as before.

N.B.—When it is not intended to re-load after firing, the command should be "Fire a volley and Shoulder;" "At *** yards, Ready." After delivering the volley make a pause, and taking the time from the right come to the Capping position, shut down the flap, bring back the hand to the "small of the butt," and in doing so close the heels; then, after another pause, taking the time from the right, come to the "Shoulder," as before detailed.

INDEPENDENT OR FILE FIRING.

Independent or File Firing may commence from the right or left of companies, or from any particular part of the line, as may be directed.

INDEPENDENT FILE FIRING FROM THE RIGHT (Left or Centre, or from both Flanks) OF COMPANIES. At this caution the rear rank will take a pace of 9 inches to the front.

COMMENCE FIRING. The flank file will at once make "Ready" and come to the "Present," the front rank man delivering his fire first, to be immediately followed by that of the rear rank man; both men will then return to the Capping position, and from thence go on with their loading in quick time, performing their motions together and without loss of time. When the flank file is bringing the rifle to the "Present," the next file is to make "Ready," coming to the "Present" when the flank file is in the act of returning to the Capping position; the next file to proceed likewise, and so continue by files in succession for the first round, after which each file, as soon as loaded, will fire independently, *i.e.*, without reference to the files either on the right or left.

TO RECEIVE CAVALRY.

CEASE FIRING. { Each file, as it completes its loading, will "Shoulder Arms." Files that may have made "Ready" when this command is given, will "half cock" their rifles and "Shoulder Arms."

NOTE.—Each man, before full cocking his rifle, is to adjust the sight for the distance he estimates the object to be from him. In File and Volley firing it is to be impressed upon the men, that the front rank must remain perfectly steady after delivering their fire, otherwise the aim of the rear rank will be deranged.

N.B.—File and Volley Firing can be conducted with greater advantage by causing the front rank to fire *kneeling* and the rear rank standing; by this means the rear rank can fire with more accuracy and safety, but the front rank must continue kneeling after "Cease Firing" until the word "Order Arms" is given.

EXERCISE TO RECEIVE CAVALRY.

The men having a thorough knowledge of the preceding portion of the drill, may now be formed into four ranks and practised to receive cavalry, as it is necessary to do in square four deep.

PREPARE TO RESIST CAVALRY. { At this caution the second and fourth ranks will take a pace of 9 inches to the front, and the whole will "Order Arms" and fix swords.

READY. { At this command the *first* and *second* ranks will sink down at once upon the right knee as a front and rear rank kneeling, in the manner prescribed when coming to the "Ready" from "Ordered Arms;" and at the same time place the butts of their rifles on the ground against the inside of their right knees, locks turned uppermost, the muzzle slanting upwards, so that the point of the sword will be about the height of a horse's nose; the left hand to have a firm grasp of the rifle immediately above the band, the right hand holding the small of the butt, the left arm to rest upon the thigh; the *third* and *fourth* ranks to make "Ready" as a front and rear rank standing, muzzles of rifles to be inclined upwards.

COMMENCE FIRING FROM THE RIGHT (or Left or from both Flanks) OF FACES.	The standing ranks to commence file firing in the order before detailed.
CEASE FIRING.	Each file, as it completes its loading, will "Shoulder Arms."
KNEELING RANKS (or Front face, &c., as the case may require) FIRE A VOLLEY.	A caution, if it be deemed necessary to fire a volley.
AT *** YDS. READY.	Come to the Capping position, at the same time bring the weight of the body on the right heel, then adjust the sight for the distance named, full cock the piece, and fix the eye steadfastly on an object in front.
PRESENT.	After delivering the fire count a pause of the slow time, and as quickly as possible bring the rifle down to resist cavalry, as before directed, remaining perfectly steady.
LOAD.	Spring to attention at the "half face," and bring the rifle to a horizontal position at the right side, seizing it at the same instant with the right hand close in front of the left, and from thence come to the position of "Prepare to Load," as standing ranks, and go on with the loading in quick time.

NOTE.—In squares of two deep, the front rank only will kneel to resist cavalry.

FORMATION OF THE COMPANY.

The Company falls in two deep, at Close order, with "Ordered Arms," the files lightly touching; it is then to "Number" from the right, and to be told off into two Subdivisions and four Sections, also "Right," "Left," for forming four deep. Should there be a blank file in telling off the Company, it will invariably be the *third* file from the left.

The Company should be sized from flanks to centre, and both ranks should be as nearly equal in height as possible.

In Close order the rear rank is closed up to within *one* pace of the front rank. In Open order they are *two* paces distant from each other; and when for Inspection, *three* paces; the pace being 30 inches, reckoning from the heels of one rank to the heels of the other rank.

Officers' Places.

The Commander of the Company takes post on the right of the front rank, covered by a Petty Officer in the rear rank. The other Officers, with the Drummer, Bugler, and Pioneers, form a third or Supernumerary rank, at *three* paces distance, the second Senior Officer standing in rear of the second file from the left.

When in Column of Subdivisions *right* in front, the Commander of the Company takes the Right Subdivision, the next Senior Officer the Left Subdivision, and *vice versa*.

When in Columns of Sections *right* in front, if four Officers are present, the Commander takes the 1st Section, the next in seniority the 3rd Section, the third in rank the 4th Section, and the junior the 2nd Section, and *vice versa*.

The proper position for the Officers being on the Pivot flanks of their respective Subdivisions or Sections.

By the term "Pivot flank" is to be understood that flank upon which Companies, Subdivisions, or Sections must be wheeled when in Column to reform line; the other is called the "Reverse Flank;" therefore when *right* in front, *left* is the Pivot, and *vice versa*.

To form Four Deep.

Fours.

Deep.
> At the word "Fours," the rear rank step back one pace.
> At the word "Deep," the left files will double behind the right files by taking a pace to the rear with the left feet, and a pace to the right with the right feet.

Fours.

About.
> At the word "Fours," the rear rank as before.
> At the word "About," the whole go to the "right about;" the left files then double as before in the proper rear of the right files, by taking a pace to the front with the right feet, and a pace to the left with the left feet.

Fours.

Right.
> At the word "Fours," the rear rank as before.
> At the word "Right," the whole face to the right; the left files then form on the right of the right files by taking a pace to the right with the right feet, and a pace to the front with the left.

Fours.

Left.
> At the word "Fours," the rear rank as before.
> At the word "Left," the whole face to the left; the left files then form on the left of the right files by taking a pace to the left with the left feet, and a pace to the rear with the right.

NOTE.—In all these formations *two* deep is re-formed from each of them by the word "Front," upon which the files move up to their respective intervals into line, the rear rank immediately closing on the front rank; the word "Halt" will precede the word "Front," if on the march. If moving to a flank, file marching may be adopted, if necessary, by the files leading out in their proper order, upon the word "Form two deep," and at the command "Form Fours" resuming their former places.

Manner of Inspecting a Company.

Attention.

Shoulder Arms. { As directed in the Manual Exercise.

For Inspection. Rear Rank take Open Order.

March.
{ The right and left hand men of the rear rank step back *two* paces, and face to their right, to mark the ground on which the rear rank is to halt.
At the word "March," they face to the front, and the rear rank step back *two* paces, dressing by their right.

Port Arms.

"Two."
{ Seize the rifle with the left hand at the lower band, raising it a few inches with the right, and slip the thumb under the cock, fingers under the guard.
Bring the rifle in the left hand to a diagonal position across the body, lock to the front, and seize the small of the butt at once with the right hand, the barrel crossing opposite the left shoulder.

Half Cock Arms. { Bring the thumb of the right hand on top of the cock, fingers behind the guard, and draw the cock back to the half cock, then grasp the small of the butt as before.

(*The Inspection of Arms is now to take place.*)

Ease Springs. { Let the cock down on the nipple, by drawing back the cock with the thumb, and trigger with the forefinger at the same time.

Shoulder Arms. { As directed in the Manual Exercise.

Order Arms. { As directed in the Manual Exercise.

Fix Swords. { As directed in the Manual Exercise.

INSPECTING A COMPANY.

EXAMINE ARMS. { Pass the rifle smartly to the left hand, which will grasp it at the upper brass, and place the butt quietly on the ground between the feet, barrel to the front; draw the ramrod with the right hand, proceeding as in the motions "Rod" and "Home" of the Platoon Exercise, then bring the right hand smartly to the right side.

When the Officer comes within one file, give the ramrod one tap to show that the rifle is not loaded, and draw it as in the motion "Return," and holding it by the middle, place it under the right arm, and on the upper brass to the left of the barrel, with the head of it to the left front.

RETURN. { Return the ramrod, and place the rifle smartly at the right side with the left hand, taking the time from the right, and resume the position of "Order Arms."

(*An Inspection of the Appointments is now to be made.*)

UNFIX SWORDS. { As directed in the Manual Exercise.

REAR RANK TAKE CLOSE ORDER. MARCH. { At the word "March" the rear rank closes within one pace.

MODE TO BE OBSERVED IN DISMISSING A COMPANY.

RIGHT FACE. LODGE ARMS. { At this order the whole "Port Arms," at the same time the front rank is to take a pace to the left, the rear rank to the right, and after a pause break off without noise.

NOTE.—In turning in a guard or picket the same mode is to be observed. On all occasions, when men return from service, the arms and accoutrements are to be carefully examined before dismissal, and all deficiences should be made good.

MOVEMENTS OF A COMPANY.

Marching to the Front.

In the drill of the Company the person instructing must always consider it as a Company in Battalion, and regulate all its movements upon that principle.

By the Right (or Left) Quick March.
{ The Instructor before he puts the Company in motion to front or rear, will indicate which flank is to direct by giving the word "By the Right" (left or centre) "Quick March;" on which eyes will be directed full to the front, and the touch preserved to the named flank, or to the centre, as required.
When the Left flank is ordered to direct, the Commander of the Company and his coverer will shift by the rear to the left of the front rank.

NOTE.—The Conductor of the Company, before the word "March" is given, will remark some distant object on the ground in his own front, and perpendicular to the directing flank, and some nearer and intermediate point in the same line, such as a stone, tuft of grass, &c., he will move upon them with accuracy, and as he approaches the nearest of those points, he must from time to time choose fresh ones in the original direction, which he will by this means preserve, never having fewer than two such points to move upon.

File Marching.

Right (or Left) Face.
{ In marching by files the Commander of the Company will lead on the inward flank of the front rank, his coverer leading the front rank; therefore, on the word "Left face," he will instantly shift to the left flank by the front and his coverer by the rear.

Quick March.
{ The whole step off together with the left foot; at the word "Halt" "Front," the Commander of the Company and his coverer return to their posts by the rear.

Wheeling forward from Line.

Company Right (or Left) Wheel.
The pivot man of the Company faces to the right (or left), and the rear rank close up; the Commander of the Company places himself one pace in front of the centre of the Company.

Quick March.
During the wheel he turns towards the men, inclining at the same time towards the pivot flank, and on completing the wheel he gives the word "Halt" "Dress."

In coming round the men look outwards, and feel inwards, stepping a shorter pace according as they are nearer to the pivot flank.

Note.—If on the march, the order would be "Right (or left) Shoulders forward," and when square "Forward."

When it is required to wheel *backwards*, the men should be faced to the "Right about."

Subdivisions (or Sections) Right (or Left) Wheel.
The pivot man of each Subdivision (or Section, faces to the right (or left), the rear rank close up; the Commander of the Company places himself one pace in front of the centre of the right (or left) Subdivision (or Section).

Quick March.
During the wheel he turns towards the men, inclining at the same time towards the pivot flank, and on completing the wheel he gives the word to the whole "Halt" "Dress."

Note.—If on the march, the order would be "Right (or left) Shoulders forward," and when square "Forward."

When in column, Divisions cover and dress to the proper pivot flank.

Wheeling into Line from Open Column of Subdivisions or Sections.

Halt.
The Company being on the march in open column of Subdivisions or Sections, "Right in Front."

COMPANY MOVEMENTS. 41

SUBDIVISIONS (or Sections) LEFT WHEEL INTO LINE. { The pivot men face to their left, and the rear rank close up. The Commander of the Company moves out, and places himself one pace in front of his Subdivision (or Section), and acts as when wheeling from line.

QUICK MARCH. { The men wheel forward, as before explained.

NOTE.—If on the march, the order would be "Right Shoulders forward;" and when in line "Forward," or "Halt," "Dress."
Wheeling into line when *left in front* is done on the same principle.

IN OPEN COLUMN OF SUBDIVISIONS, OR SECTIONS TO CHANGE DIRECTION ON THE MARCH.

CHANGE DIRECTION TO THE RIGHT (or Left). { The Commander of the leading Subdivision will give the word "Left (or right) Shoulders forward," and when his Subdivision has wheeled square to that direction, he will give the word "Forward." The leader of the second Subdivision, when he arrives at the ground where the first began to change its direction, will give the same words, following the exact tract, and always preserving his distance from the Division in his front.

TO COUNTERMARCH BY FILES.

RIGHT (or Left) FACE. LEFT (or Right) COUNTERMARCH. { The Commander of the Company takes one pace outwards, facing inwards, ready to halt the Company, his coverer facing to the "Right about."

QUICK MARCH. { The whole step off together, and the leading file, wheeling short round on the front rank, proceeds, followed by the Company in file till it reaches the coverer, when the Commander gives the word "Halt," "Front," "Dress."

NOTE.—In Countermarching by Files, the Instructor must consider the Company as a Division of a Battalion in Column; he will, therefore, signify beforehand whether the *Right* or *Left* is supposed to be in front, that the Commander and his coverer may be placed on the Pivot flank, as it is a rule that the facings be made from the Flank then the Pivot one, to the one which is to become such.

To Countermarch by Ranks.

Right & Left Face. Right Countermarch.
The front rank faces to the right the rear rank to the left.

Quick March.
The whole step off together, the two ranks severally wheeling in single file till the pivot man of the front rank comes close to the coverer, when the Commander gives the word "Halt," "Front," "Dress."

From Open Column of Subd^{ns} halted (*right in front*) to form Line to the Front.

Form Company.
At this order the Commander of the Company gives the word "Left Subdivision, Left half face," "Quick March." He will then move to where the left of his Company will rest, and when the Left Subdivision is in line with the rear rank of the Right Subdivision, he gives the word "Halt," "Front," "Dress up."

NOTE.—If on the march, the Commander will give the word "Left Subdivision, Left half turn," "Double," and afterwards "Front turn," "Quick."
Forming line when *left in front* is done on the same principle.

From Line halted to form Column of Subdivisions (*right in front.*)

Form Subdivisions.
The Officer of the Left Subdivision falls back to mark the point where the left flank is to rest.
The Commander of the Company gives the word "Left Subdivision, Right about three-quarters face," "Quick March." The Officer of the Left Subdivision when the Pivot file reaches him gives the word "Halt," "Front," "Dress."

NOTE.—If on the march, the Commander would give the word Left Subdivision, "Mark time," "Right half turn;" and when it is properly behind the Right Subdivision, the Officer gives the word "Front turn."
Forming Column of Subdivisions *left in front* is done on the same principle.
The same directions that are given for forming line or column by Subdivisions apply equally to Sections.

COMPANY MOVEMENTS. 43

FORMING COMPANIES, SUBDIVISIONS, OR SECTIONS FROM FILE MARCHING (*right in front*).

FRONT FORM COMPY. (Subdivisions or Sections.) — At this order the front rank man of the leading file marks time, the remainder make a whole face to the left, and wheel to the right, looking outwards and feeling inwards *i.e.*, if right in front, turn to the left, and if left in front, turn to the right.

FORWARD. — This order is given as soon as the quarter circle is complete if the march is to be continued, but if not, "Halt," "Dress."

NOTE.—The Company marching in file has only to "Halt," and "Front," to be formed to the left or right flank, according as the right or left is in front.

RIGHT FORM COMPANY. — At this order the front rank man of the leading file will wheel to the right, take one pace to the front and halt; the rear rank moving round, and covering; the remainder of the Company, form on the left of the right file, by files in succession.

RIGHT ABOUT FORM COMPANY. — At this order the leading file wheels to the "right about" and takes one pace to the front after wheeling; the remainder of the Company march on in file, wheeling round the halted file, and forming on its left by files in succession; each file as it comes into the line taking up its dressing from the standing flank.

NOTE.—Forming company to the "Left," and "Left about" when *left in front*, is done on the same principle.

The directions detailing the various formations from File Marching are also applicable to "Fours." On the command "Front form Company," or "Right form Company," the Company will instantly form two deep, and proceed as in file.

When moving by "Fours," and a change of direction is required, the command will be as in File Marching, "Right Wheel," or "Left Wheel."

File Marching can be re-formed from column of Subdivisions or Sections on the march, by simply giving the order, when *right* in front, "Right Turn," "Left Wheel;" or when *left* in front, "Left Turn," "Right Wheel."

To form Line to either Flank from Open Column of Subdivisions (*right in front*).

The Company may be formed to the left flank, by wheeling into line, as before explained; but when it is desired to form to the *right* flank, it must be done as follows:—

Right Form Company.
The leaders of the several divisions shift by the rear to the right flank, the Commander of the right Subdivision then gives the word to his division "Left Shoulders forward;" and when square, "Forward," till he has gained three paces, then "Halt," "Dress."

The second Subdivision when it has arrived at the left flank of the first, its Commander, falling to the rear, gives the word "Left Shoulders forward," "Forward," then "Halt," "Dress up," on which the division moves up in line with the one formed.

NOTE.—Forming to either flank when *left in front* is done on the same principle.

To form the Rallying Square.

Form the Rallying Square.
The Instructor of the drill having caused the Company to disperse to a certain distance, will give the word "Form the Rallying Square," at the same time placing himself facing the supposed enemy; the men hasten to the person so posted, fixing swords, and ordering their arms as they reach him.

The two first who join him form on his right and left, facing outwards. The three next place themselves in front of those posted, and three others to the rear facing to the rear, thus forming a square of three. The instructor will cause the next four men to take post at the several angles; and others as they come up will complete the different faces between these angles, which will form a square of five.

The square may then be augmented in the same manner to a square of seven, or nine, four deep, by the angles being occupied by four more men, and the faces filled up as before; and the square will then be composed of eighty men.

When the Square is to March.

The Square will move to the Front (Rear, Right, or Left). Inwards Face. Quick March.

In order to move with the necessary regularity, previously to putting the square in motion, the instructor will cause the faces to be dressed; and after the caution, he will give the words "Inwards Face," and it will face in the named direction, and step off accordingly at the word "Quick March."

To Resist Cavalry.

Halt. Prepare to resist Cavalry. Ready.

Upon the word "Halt," the square will halt and face outwards; and when it is to "Prepare to resist Cavalry," upon the word "Ready," the front rank only (if the square is two or three deep) will kneel; if four deep, the two front ranks will kneel.

If ordered to fire, the standing ranks only will commence an independent fire in the order detailed for File Firing.

Reduce the Square. Quick March.

On the word "Quick March," the men open out, and fall in, in their proper places.

NOTE.—In this manner, small dispersed parties, from eight to eighty men, may be formed to resist an attack of cavalry in an open country, where, from whatever cause, they may have separated from the column of march. Boats' crews should also be taught to form in the same manner when required.

When a Company, or other small body, in close files, requires to form to resist cavalry, it may be wheeled forward into column of Sections and closed to the front. When halted, the two rear Sections face to the "right about," and the two outward files of the second and third Sections face to their right and left, so as to present a front in all directions. The men in the angles also face to their right and left.

FIELD EXERCISE FOR A BATTALION OF SEAMEN.

Formation of the Battalion.

THE Companies will draw up according to number, viz., 1, 2, 3, &c., from right to left, and there is to be no interval between any of them; the Battalion will then be told off into right and left Wings, the Companies being previously told off, as in Company drill.

Officers' Places, &c.

The Commanding Officer is the only officer advanced in front for the purpose of Exercise; but on the March in line, and in the Firings, he is in rear of the centre.

The Commander of each Company is on the right of the front rank of his Company when in line, covered by a Petty Officer in the rear rank, and on the pivot flank when in column. The second Senior Officer of the Left Company is on the left of the Battalion; the remaining Officers form a third or Supernumerary rank at three paces distance when in line, but at one pace distance when in column.

In the firings the Commanders of Companies drop to the rear; and whenever they move out of the front rank their places are taken by their coverers and preserved till the Officers again resume them.

The essential use of the Supernumerary rank is to keep the others closed up to the front during the attack, and to prevent any break in the rear; and to bring up a fresh supply of ammunition if required.

The pioneers from each Company are assembled two deep behind the centre of the Right Company, and nine paces in rear of the Supernumerary rank.

The drummers, fifers, and buglers are assembled in two divisions in line with the pioneers, one division being in rear of the 2nd Company, the other in rear of the 2nd Company

BATTALION DRILL. 47

from the left. When in column, the pioneers, drummers, and buglers are on the reverse flank, except when "Marching past in Review Order," when they lead at the head of the Column.

On the Battalion being formed, the Commanding Officer will give the Order for 6 Companies, as follows:—

NUMBER YOUR DIVISIONS.
{ At this order the Commanders of Companies will take a pace to the front, face to the left, and tell off their Companies in succession, as follows:—
The Officer of No. 1 calling "No. 1." "Right Flank Company Right Wing."
The Officer of No. 2 calling " No. 2." "Right Wing."
The Officer of No. 3 calling "No. 3." "Right Centre Company Right Wing."
The Officer of No. 4 calling " No. 4." " Left Centre Company Left Wing."
The Officer of No. 5 calling "No. 5." " Left Wing."
The Officer of No. 6 calling " No. 6." " Left Flank Company Left Wing." }

FALL IN. { The Officers take up their posts as before.

MANŒUVRES.

Marching in Line.

When an advance is made in line, the Companies of the right wing must preserve the touch to their left; and those of the left wing the touch to their right; the advance being regulated by the centre.

The Line will advance. { On this caution the rear rank will lock up.

Quick March. { The whole line instantly steps off, the eyes directed full to the front.

Halt. { On the order "Halt," the rear rank at all times take a shortened pace.

To change Front to a Flank from Line.

Change Front to the Right on No. 1. "No. 1 the Q^r Circle Remaining Companies 4 Paces Right Wheel." Quick March. { The leader of No. 1 wheels his Company a quarter circle to the right, and halts.
The remaining Companies are halted by their leaders when they have wheeled the four paces.

Line on No. 1. Quick March. { The remaining Companies, as they respectively arrive on the new alignment receive the words from their leaders "Left Shoulders forward," "Halt," "Dress up."

Note.—Changing front to the *left* is done on the same principle.
When changing front on the Centre Company, *one* wing must be faced to the Right about."

Changing Front to the Right on No. 1 Company.

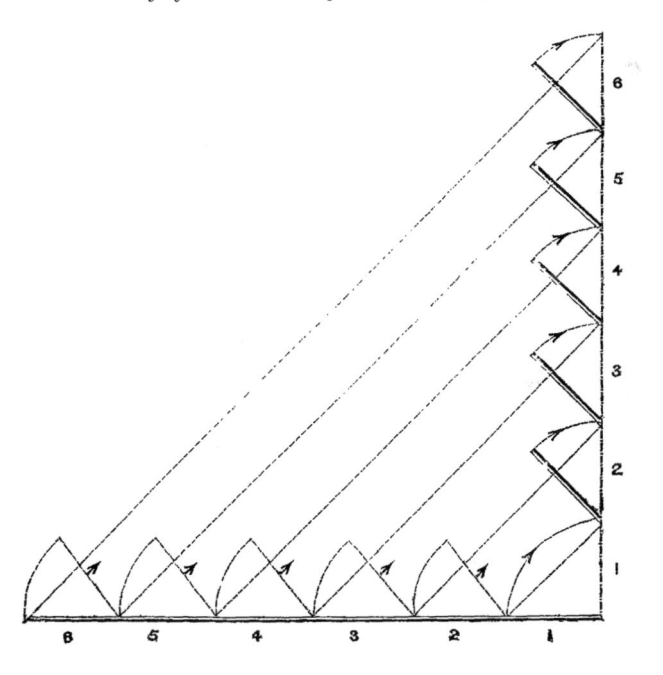

Breaking into Open Column RIGHT *in Front.*

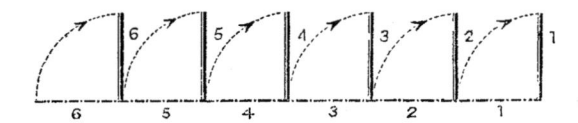

Breaking into Open Column LEFT *in Front.*

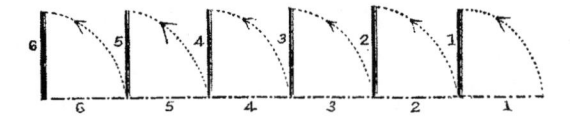

Breaking into Open Column.

Open Column Right in Front. Divisions Left Shoulders Forward.

When in line, and it becomes necessary to break into Open Column, it is to be done (if right in front) by bringing left shoulders forward, when the right hand man of each Company will mark time, the remainder bringing their left shoulders forward, looking to their left and feeling into their right; the Officer of each Company passes by the front to the left flank, and gives the words "Halt," "Dress," when wheeled square.

Open Column Left in Front. Divisions Right Shoulders Forward.

The left hand men mark time, and the remainder bring their right shoulders forward, looking to their right and feeling to their left; Officers remain on the right flank, and wheel with the Company, giving the words "Halt," "Dress," when wheeled square.

Forming Close or Quarter Distance Column.

Form close (or Q^r.Distance) Column on No. —

Close or Quarter distance Column is formed by the leading Company receiving the order from the Officer to "Halt," and the remaining Companies the same order on arriving at Close, Quarter, or Half distance; or it may be formed by the march of Companies to a flank from line, when it is intended to form in rear of the right or left Company.

When Close Column is formed, the Companies must be at *two* paces distance, measuring from the heels of the rear rank to the heels of the front rank.

Note.—The Column at Quarter distance is applicable to most changes of position, except formation of line to a flank, or where line is to be formed to a new front. In all route marches the Quarter distance Column should be adopted; it unites the convenience of moving upon a space three-fourths less than the extent occupied by the march of an Open Column.

The wheel of a Column at Close distance on a fixed pivot is the simplest method of changing front to a flank.

Close or Quarter Distance Column wheeling to the Right or Left.

Column to the Right (or Left) Wheel. — Upon the caution (if *right in front*), the flank file on the right (or left) of the front Company, whether Officer or man, will face to the right (or left); the front Company stands fast, but the remaining Companies make a "half face" to the left (or right).

Quick March. — Upon the word "Quick March," the front Company will wheel as usual, with the exception that the step must be much shorter, and so regular as to give the rear Companies time to come round. These Companies will step off at the same moment, bringing their left (or right) shoulders gradually up, and each file circling round and covering the relative files of the Company in front. The Officers will circle in the same way round the Officers in their front.

Halt. — The Commanding Officer will give the word "Halt," when he sees the leading Company has completed the wheel, at which time the rear Companies must also have circled round in the new direction.

Note.—If on the march, the order would be, "Column will wheel to the right (or left)," "Left (or right) Shoulders forward," when the companies will face and move as before, the leading company advancing at a very short pace in the new direction until the word "Forward," or "Halt," is given.

To form Open Column from Close or Quarter Distance halted.

Open out wheeling dist. from the Rear. Quick March. — The whole, except the rear Company, step off, and each Company, when at its proper wheeling distance, is halted by the Leader of the Company immediately in its rear.

Close Column Wheeling to the Right.

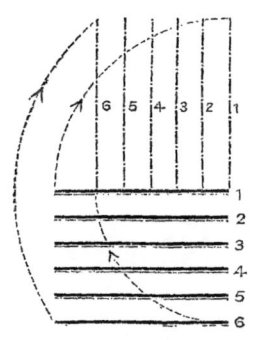

From Open Column RIGHT *in Front to form Line to the Left Flank.*

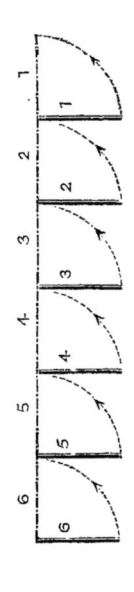

From Open Column RIGHT *in Front to form Line to the Right Flank.*

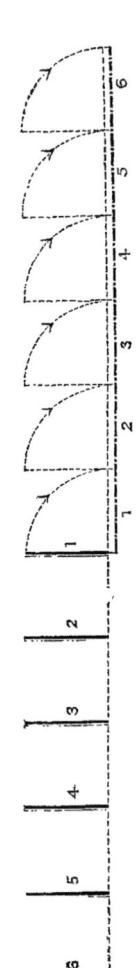

BATTALION DRILL

OPEN OUT WHEELING DIST. FROM THE FRONT. "Remaining Companies Right about face." QUICK MARCH.
> The whole, except the front Company, face to the "right about."
> The whole, except the front Company, step off, and each Company, when at its proper wheeling distance, receives the word from its own Leader.
> No. — "Halt," "Front," "Dress."

OPEN OUT WHEELING DIST. FROM THE CENTRE. QUICK MARCH.
> This is a combination of the two preceding methods.

TO FORM LINE TO EITHER FLANK FROM OPEN COLUMN HALTED (*Right in front*).

To form Line to the Left Flank.

DIVISIONS LEFT WHEEL INTO LINE. QUICK MARCH.
> Each Company wheels on its pivot, and is halted when in line by its Leader.

NOTE.—If on the march, the order would be, "Divisions Right Shoulders forward," and when square, "Halt," or "Forward."
Wheeling into line when *left in front* is done on the same principle.

To form Line to the Right Flank.

FORM LINE TO THE RIGHT ON THE LEADING DIVISION. QUICK MARCH.
> The Leader of No. 1 gives the word "Left Shoulders Forward," and when square, "Forward" three paces, then "Halt," "Dress."
> The Leader of No. 2, when in line with the left flank of No. 1, gives the word "Left Shoulders Forward," and when square, "Forward," till in line with rear rank of No. 1, then "Halt," "Dress up."
> The other Divisions continue the march, and wheel in succession in the same manner.

NOTE.—If on the march, the same orders would be given, excepting the word "Quick March."
Forming line when *left in front* is done on the same principle.

E 2

Deploying into Line on the "Front," "Rear," or "Centre" Company, from Close or Quarter Distance Column.

Deploy on No. —
{ The caution being given to Deploy, if on the front Company it stands fast, if on the rear or centre, the Company of formation will be moved up in double time to the ground occupied by the leading Company the moment its front is clear.

Remaining Companies outwards face.

Quick March.
{ At the word "Quick March," the remaining companies step off, moving parallel to the line of formation.

The Officer of the Company immediately in rear of the leading one stands fast, and allows his Company to move onwards, a space equal to that which it occupies in line; he then gives the word "Front Turn," and, when within *one* pace of the line, "Halt," "Dress up;" each of the succeeding Company Officers, when he hears the word "Front turn" given to the Company on his inward flank, "Halts," in the same manner, and gives the same orders to his Company, when they have gained their proper distance.

After dressing their Companies, the Officers resume their places on the right of their Companies in line.

Deploying into Line on the Front Company

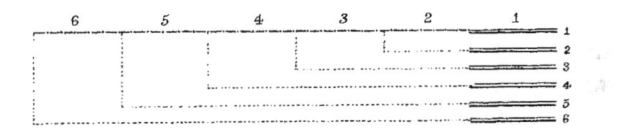

Deploying into Line on a Central Company.

Forming Square on the leading Division from Open Column.

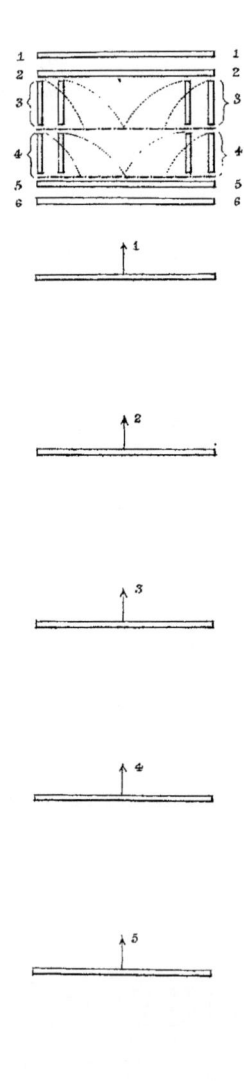

To form a Square Four Deep.

First form Open or Quarter Distance Column.

The Comm^g. Officer will then give the order, if at *open* column.

Form Square on the Leading Division. Quick March.

The front Company stands fast, the next Company closes, receiving the word from its Leader, No. —; "Halt," "Dress;" the other Companies, except the two rear ones, close up to Section distance, receiving the words from their Leaders, "Sections outwards," upon which the Companies wheel outwards, the rear Sections closing on the front, and halt when wheeled square.

The two rear Companies close, and receive the words from their Leaders "Halt," "Right about face," the Officers and Supernumeraries forming in the centre. The Square may now be moved or halted to resist Cavalry, &c., as before detailed with a Rallying square.

Note.—Forming Square from Q^r. Dist. Column is done in the same manner, except that the Comm^g. Officer gives the word "Sections Outwards" as soon as the Second Comp^y. has closed on the Leading one.

Re-form Column. Quick March.

At this order the rear Sections of the side faces step back in slow time.

The front Company advances Section distance, and the central Companies wheel back, receiving from their Leaders "Halt," "Dress." The second Company stands fast, and the two rear Companies retire to Quarter distance, receiving from their Leaders "Halt," "Front," "Dress;" the Supernumeraries fall into their places as before, and the Column is wheeled or deployed as required.

Note.—The foregoing Manœuvres are all that are considered necessary for the handling of a body of Seamen; they should, however, be practised to work in inverted order, but all unnecessary and complicated movements should be avoided.

LIGHT INFANTRY MOVEMENTS.

The following Light Infantry Movements established in the Army, will be found a Useful Guide for Seamen.

DETAIL OF FORMATION.

When Seamen are drilled by word of command, they move at the *last* word, which should be given short.

"Paces—From the Right—Extend."
"Paces—From the Centre—Extend," &c.
"To the Right—Close," &c.
"Advance—Halt—Fire—Retire," &c.

Companies should often be practised in judging their own distance of files; the points on which the flanks are to rest being previously notified.

To Extend from the Halt.
{ As soon as the order is given (either by word of command, or by bugle), the Officer commanding drops to the rear, placing himself in rear of the centre; the next Officer in rear of the right, and the third Officer in rear of the left. At the last sound of the bugle, the named file stands fast, and *drops on the knee* in the Capping position; the remainder "shoulder arms," face, and extend in quick time, unless ordered to move at the double march.

The front rank men of files move straight before them, covering correctly on the march; their respective rear rank men cast their eye over the inward shoulder, and tap their front rank men, at the distance of two, four, six, or any other given number of paces, as a signal for them to "halt," "front," and *drop on the knee* in the Capping position.

LIGHT INFANTRY MOVEMENTS. 55

DISTANCE OF FILES.
> The paces are indicated by the previous caution of the Commanding Officer; but if no number is specified, *six* paces is the regulated distance between the files. If the distance between the files be not correct, it must not be altered by closing or opening out.

TO FIRE IN EXTENDED ORDER ON THE SPOT.
> So soon as the "Fire" has sounded, the front rank men will make "Ready" and fire, and commence loading; and the rear rank men, when their front rank men are in the act of Capping, will make "Ready" and fire, and afterwards load.

TO CEASE FIRING.
> After the bugle sounds the "Cease," every loaded musket must be carefully *half cocked*, and not a shot heard; the unloaded men re-load as rapidly as possible, and the whole remain steady, ready to move.

TO FIRE LYING.
> The caution to "Lie down," is repeated by the Officers; and when the bugle sounds the "Fire," the whole drop on *both knees* (the rear rank men disengaging), and throw themselves on their bellies. The firing proceeds as before. When at the "Present," both elbows to be on the ground, to support both the body and the rifle. The men load on their knees.
>
> Riflemen may fire on their backs in favourable situations; in this position, the feet are crossed, the right foot passing through the sling of the rifle, and the piece supported by it. It furnishes a steady aim with a short rifle. If in a very exposed situation the Seaman attempts to load lying, he will roll over on his back, and, placing the butt between his legs, the lock upwards, and the muzzle a little elevated, draw his ramrod, and go on with his loading without exposure, rolling over on his breast again when ready to fire. When firing in this position, great care should be taken by the men that they do not drop their ammunition out of their pouches.

THE LINE WILL ADVANCE.	At the last sound of the bugle to "Advance," the whole rise up, and step off in quick time, keeping their distances from the centre.
THE LINE WILL RETIRE.	At the last sound of the bugle, the whole go to the "left about," and retire together, rear rank leading.
TO FIRE ADVANCING.	At this signal the front-rank man of each file fires, and instantly drops to the rear by the *left* of his comrade, and loads upon the march, holding the rifle as upright as possible, giving the word "Ready," when in the act of Capping, in an under tone of voice; on which the other man fires, and proceeds in the same manner, taking care that both men are never unloaded at the same time. The men must cover their file leaders, who, without withdrawing their attention from the object in their front, can with a glance of the eye avoid losing distance, or getting before or behind the file next to them towards their centre. When firing advancing, the men may *kneel* to fire, their comrade or file leader kneeling also.

NOTE.—Unless much exposed, it is better to load *standing*, accordingly the men after firing may drop to the rear, and halt to load, running up to their file leaders (who continue moving on), when loaded, and giving the word "Ready" as before—so on alternately. In parade practice, however, on open ground, it is desirable that the men should always go through the motions on the march, as it tends to make them expert and handy with their arms. This is not to apply to *ball practice*, in which the men are to *stand* to load and run up.

TO FIRE RETIRING.	If in motion, the whole halt; the front-rank men give their fire, turn to the "left about," and move straight to the rear, loading on the march. When their loading is completed, they will "halt," "front," and *kneel down*, in the position of making "Ready," adjust their sight for the distance, and full cock. Then the rear rank men (who had *kneeled down* when their front rank men retired) will fire, and retire at the double, in the same

LIGHT INFANTRY MOVEMENTS.

To Fire Retiring (*continued*).

manner, carrying their rifles in their left hands, and passing to the *proper left* of their front rank men, when they will resume the quick time and commence their loading, holding the rifle as upright as possible. As soon as they have loaded, they will "halt," "front," and *kneel*, as before.

Thus the ranks continue to retire alternately, as soon as the ramrods of the rank that has retired are done working. In the field, however, the distance to be taken by each rank in retreating will depend upon the movements of the enemy, the nature of the ground, and other circumstances; but when cover presents itself at hand, the men should always avail themselves of it.

Halt.

At this signal, if "advancing," the Skirmishers *kneel down*, taking advantage of any inequalities of the ground in their neighbourhood, and continuing to fire until the "Cease firing" has sounded. If the Skirmishers "are retiring," the rank next the enemy will stand fast (or face "about" if not already fronting towards the enemy), and the other rank closes up to it, *kneeling down;* and the whole continue firing, taking care that both ranks are never unloaded at the same time.

To Close.

On the signal being sounded, the men rise up, "trail arms," face to the point required, close in quick time, and "order arms." *If on the march*, the named file moves steadily on, the remainder make a "half turn," and close in double time.

To Extend while a Division is advancing; from the Centre, Right or Left.

In all these cases, the files from which the extension takes place move straight forward in quick time; the others make a "half turn" to the flank to which they are ordered to extend, and move off at double time. As soon as each file has got its regular distance, it will turn to the front, and advance, resuming the quick time; rear rank men covering their front rank men, and keeping in line with the directing file.

58   LIGHT INFANTRY MOVEMENTS.

To Incline to the Right or Left

Advance.

The Skirmishers make a "half turn" to the flanks to which they are ordered to incline (rear rank men covering their front rank men), and continue in the diagonal direction, until the "Advance" is sounded, when they will return to their original front, and move forward as before. If, when the Skirmishers have made the "half-turn," the bugle should sound the "Incline" a *second* time, the men's shoulders should be brought up, so as to complete the face and march in file.

To Halt from the Incline.

At this signal the whole "front," and *kneel down*, continuing to fire till the signal to "Cease firing" has sounded.

Change Front to the Right, on the Right File. Double March.

The right file faces to the right, kneeling; the others rise up and "trail," and make a right or left "half face;" at the word "Double march," they form on the right file. The distance will be preserved from the halted flank. Each file will move in the shortest line to its situation in the new position, and instantly *kneel down*.

Right or Left Shoulders Forward.

But in throwing a wing backward or forward, the distance of files must be preserved from the inward flank, and they must look to the outward flank for dressing, and bring forward the shoulders gradually, conformably to its progress.

Change Front on the Left File, Right thrown back. Double March.

The left hand file faces to the *right*, kneeling; the others rise up, "trail," and face to the "left about three-quarters;" step off at the double march, and when in line, face "about" and *kneel*.

SKIRMISHING.

A Company or Companies may extend by files from any part of the line, and at various distances, as may be ordered; and it is a rule that the men of a file invariably act together, to inspire confidence, and to afford mutual protection and support.

Detached Skirmishers. Detached Skirmishers are governed by circumstances and situation; they must never, however, get too far in advance, so as to expose their flanks, but must regulate their movements by the files upon their right and left. They will fire either standing, kneeling, or lying, as the case may require, ever bearing in mind that the grand requisites in skirmishing are a sure, quick, and steady aim, together with that ready tact in seizing at a glance those local advantages which enable a man to do the utmost injury to his enemy with the least exposure to himself.

General Line of Skirmishers. In the field, Skirmishers advance in a general line, pushing on or falling back, from post to post, and never standing exposed, even for an instant, when there is cover of any kind at hand. It is therefore always proper, when obliged to advance, across an open space, upon an enemy posted under cover, to make a quick and simultaneous rush towards the point; a regular and systematic advance across such ground, however resolutely conducted, would entail a great and very useless sacrifice of lives.

To Advance in a General Line Firing.

At the signal to "Fire," the front rank man of each file fires and instantly drops to the rear by the *left* of his comrade, and loads as quickly as he can upon the march, giving the word "Ready," when loaded, as the signal for his file leader (who has continued leading on), to fire. As often, however, as cover of any kind presents itself within reach, each file, in mutual concert, will make for it, one man running on while his comrade covers his advance by aiming at the enemy and distracting his attention; he then in turn runs forward, when the cover is secured, and both continue to fire from the spot as long as circumstances may sanction; always remembering that the great object in advancing is to drive back the enemy's skirmishers rapidly on their reserves, giving them no time for rallying or making a stand.

To Retire Firing.

On a plain, the Skirmishers may retire by *alternate ranks*, as before described, but whenever the country is at all wooded, broken, or inclosed, it will always be advisable to retire in a general line, trusting to the skill of the Officer, and the firmness and intelligence of the men for disputing it successfully. Before falling back, the Skirmisher should scan the ground he is to traverse, and having selected his next station, he will make for it with the utmost expedition.

When a line of Skirmishers is hard pressed, there is no better way of giving them relief, and at the same time of offering resistance to the enemy, than by extending the Supports as often as a line of defence presents itself, the old Skirmishers passing quickly through the new line, forming into Supports: again, in turn extending, and so on alternately. Even on a plain this will be the best mode of disputing the ground; the Supports, after extending, should *lie down* until the Skirmishers have passed through them.

NOTE.—Either in advancing or retiring, it may be better to do it by *alternate files*, instead of ranks, as then comrades are not separated in danger.

SKIRMISHING. 61

ACCURATELY DRESSED LINES NO OBJECT IN SKIRMISHING.
Accurately dressed lines are not an object in skirmishing. The men must be guided by the nature of the ground they are acting on; all that can be desired on this head is, that the files should be so placed as to support, and fire clear of each other.

GENERAL RULE FOR LOADING.
It is a rule that both men of a file are never unloaded at the same time; that they always load, when practicable, under cover, and *standing*, previous to moving in advance, and after falling back in retreat, from one spot to another.

ALL UNNECESSARY BUGLING TO BE AVOIDED.
It will often be prudent to communicate orders to a line of Skirmishers by passing them along the rear, instead of betraying an intended movement by the bugle. For the "retreat" to one party is the "advance" to their opponents, who are generally well acquainted with the sounds and prepared to act upon them.

GENERAL RULE FOR THE MOVEMENT OF SUPPORTS.
The Supports advance and retire generally in line, except when threatened with Cavalry, when they will move in close column of Sections; and Skirmishers, in running in on a Support, form up in Sections in its rear. Supports move to a flank in column of Sections.

SKIRMISHERS TO OVERLAP THE FLANKS OF LINES.
In covering the advance of lines, Skirmishers will take care to protect and overlap the flanks.

RELIEVING SKIRMISHERS WHEN HALTED.
In relieving a line of Skirmishers, the new line extends in the rear, out of reach of the enemy's fire, and afterwards runs up to the old line; each file of the former proceeding rapidly to the rear, under the protecting fire of the new line, and when out of reach of the enemy's fire, they close in upon their Supports. But should an immediate advance be intended, the relieved Skirmishers ought to remain in the line *lying down*, instead of exposing themselves to a fire whilst retiring.

62 SKIRMISHING.

RELIEVING WHEN ADVANCING. — If the relief takes place while advancing, the new Skirmishers will run up in the same way, and pass briskly in front of the others; the old skirmishers *lie down* till they are out of the enemy's fire, after which they close upon their Supports as before.

RELIEVING WHEN RETIRING. — If relieving while retiring, the new Skirmishers extend a considerable distance in the rear, and each man looks out for a good situation. The old Skirmishers continue to retire in their usual order until within twenty or thirty paces of the former; they then run through them to the rear, until they are out of reach of the enemy's fire, after which they close.

GENERAL RULE TO BE OBSERVED IN SKIRMISHING AT A DISTANCE FROM THE COLUMN OR LINE. — If a Company be directed to skirmish at a distance, detached from the timely support of the Column or line, one general principle must be observed, namely, that never more than *one-half* must be sent forward to skirmish at a time; the other half remains formed and ready to support.

HOW THE UNITY OF COMPANIES WHEN SKIRMISHING IS BEST PRESERVED. — When *more* than one Company is employed in skirmishing, one Company should skirmish and another support. Unnecessary division of parts is always objectionable.

SKIRMISHERS TO CLEAR THE FRONT OF THE BATTALION WHEN THE ASSEMBLY SOUNDS. — When a Company is skirmishing in front of a Battalion, and the "Assembly" sounds, it is of the utmost consequence that the front of the Battalion should be left clear as soon as possible.

HOW TO RUN IN ON THE BATTALION. — The Skirmishers, therefore, if detached to any distance, must endeavour instantly to discover the exact situation of the Battalion, and decide in what direction to run in, adopting that mode which will least impede, and soonest leave it in a situation for firing or advancing.

SKIRMISHING.

IF NOT CALLED IN.
If the Skirmishers *are not called in*, while the Battalion performs any movement, they must, with the utmost rapidity, change their situation, so as to correspond with the new order of the Battalion; and their attention and activity are chiefly required in protecting it during the change.

FORMATION OF SQUARE.
When the Battalion forms Square, the Skirmishers will take the most direct and short way to the rear, and close up and compose the *rear* face.

RALLYING SQUARE.
The "Alarm" followed by the "Assembly" will be sounded on the first appearance of the enemy's Cavalry, when, if there is no cover within reach, and not sufficient time to form on the Support, the Skirmishers will form the "Rallying Square," the Officer on whom it forms taking care so to station himself for its formation as not to cloud the front of the Support; or if no alternative is left, a few men back to back should show a bold front, which, in many cases, if the men are steady, is sufficient to keep off Cavalry.

RALLYING SQUARE NEED NOT BE FORMED WHEN COVER IS AT HAND.
But when there is cover near, such as a hedge, ditch, copse, &c., the Skirmishers should at once make for it, and aid the Supports by a cross fire.

ADVANCE GUARD.

General Intention of Advanced Guards.

Advanced guards are formed for the purpose of feeling the way through a country in front of a Column, to gain intelligence of the enemy, and to give timely notice of his vicinity or approach, in order that the Main body may have time to prepare either for making or repelling an attack; and, as a general rule, no body of men should move without an Advance Guard.

Precautions to be observed in approaching a Village.

An Advanced guard on approaching a village must proceed with great precaution if feeling for an enemy. The Reserve and Advanced parties on the road must be halted beyond the reach of musketry from the village, while strong flanking parties are sent round the outskirts so as to threaten the rear. The Petty officer's party on the road may then move on in single files, with a considerable interval between them, followed by as many files in succession from the Support as may be deemed expedient; and the Supports and Reserve will move forward when it has been ascertained that the place is not in the occupation of the enemy.

The leading files should be instructed that the first object to be sought for in a village is the Church, from the belfry of which a view of the surrounding country may be gained.

Similar Precautions to be observed previous to entering a Defile or Hollow Way.

The head of an Advanced guard must never commit itself by entering a defile or hollow way without previously occupying the heights on either side by flanking parties. When the heights are thus crowned, the leading party on the road will send on a single file, which will be followed by others in succession, near enough to keep the preceding one in view; the flanking parties on either hand continuing to precede the centre until the defile is passed, when they will gradually fall back to their former stations, and the whole move forward in the original formation.

ADVANCE GUARD.

GENERAL RULE IN APPROACHING VILLAGES, WOODS, &c. — That woods, villages, and generally every object capable of affording concealment to an enemy, should invariably be turned, and the rear threatened previous to being felt in front.

COMMANDER OF AN ADVANCED GUARD TO OBSERVE EVERYTHING HIMSELF, AND TO BE DISTINCT IN HIS REPORTS. — The Officer commanding an Advanced guard should endeavour to observe everything himself, taking especial care that any reports he may have to make are clear, decided, and correct.

CONDUCT OF DETACHED PARTIES IN FALLING IN WITH AN ENEMY. — No specific rules can be laid down for the conduct of an Advanced guard in every case of falling in with an enemy. It cannot, however, be too strongly impressed on all employed on services of this nature, that nothing is more dangerous or reprehensible than offensive or defensive measures undertaken in an isolated manner; Advanced parties and Patrols should never, therefore, be suffered to engage of their own accord, if it can possibly be avoided.

ADVANCED GUARDS SHOULD INVARIABLY RE-FORM AFTER DISLODGING AN ENEMY. — No Advanced guard or detached party of any kind, after carrying a post, should ever be permitted to advance without re-forming. The men should on no account pursue the flying enemy, but re-form rapidly, and wait for further orders.

F

PATROLS.

Strength. The employment and judicious management of Patrols form an essential part of the precautionary duties of an Advanced guard. They may consist of a Junior Officer's party; a Petty Officer and twelve, or a Petty Officer and six men, according to circumstances.

Utility of Patrols. The object of a Patrol is to obtain intelligence, and to ascertain the presence of an enemy. They are detached to examine houses, copses, enclosures, &c., near the line of march, capable of affording concealment to the enemy, and too distant to be inspected by the advanced or flanking parties. All heights from which a view of the surrounding country can be obtained, should also be ascended by Patrols, precaution being used to see everything, if possible, without being seen.

REAR GUARD.

General Intention of Rear Guard. A Rear guard is an Advanced guard reversed; it covers the retreating column from any sudden assault in the rear, and it prevents the enemy from stealing round, and gaining on the flanks of the main body. The prevention of straggling is also an important part of the duties of a Rear guard.

When embarking in boats, the Rear guard should cover the embarkation.

N.B.—When an Advanced or Rear guard is marching along a road, &c., the different parties should never lose sight of those either in front or rear of them, for which purpose, in *turning an angle*, a man should *invariably* be left till the next party approaches.

By a neglect of this precaution, part of an Advanced or Rear guard might be cut off without the remainder being aware of it.

EXTRACTS FROM THE
"INSTRUCTION OF MUSKETRY" FOR THE ARMY,

For the Guidance of Instructors of Rifle Drill on Board Ship.

1. *The Instructor should teach the men that, to aim with accuracy, it is necessary that the sights should be carefully aligned between the eye and the mark.* If the sights, however, on the upper surface of the barrel were so constructed as to be parallel to the axis, as on a great gun, it would then be necessary, at 100 yards, to aim 1 foot 5 inches above the mark; but in so doing the firer would lose sight of the object, and he would, besides, be uncertain of his correct elevation. The height of the lowest back sight is therefore so arranged, that when aim is taken straight upon an object at 100 yards, the axis of the piece receives the necessary elevation.

2. The effect of wind should be next shown; when blowing from the right it will blow the bullet towards the left of the mark, and *vice versâ;* when from the front it will slightly *reduce* the range of the bullet, and when from the rear *increase* it; the man should, however, be cautioned that a front or rear wind does not produce so much effect as a side wind, and that he must be guided entirely by his own experience in making allowance for wind, as no fixed rules can be laid down for his guidance. If the wind, for instance, is blowing from the left, he must aim a little to the left of the mark; if he finds that the shot still strikes to the right, he must make a little more allowance.

3. The rifled barrel is cut by three spiral grooves (here the man should be made to look through the barrel and observe the grooves), constructed in such a manner that the groove which is on the left side at the breech makes a half turn over the barrel, and appears on the right side of the muzzle; so the other two grooves make a half turn in the barrel, passing over from left to right.

4. When the bullet is expanded by the explosion of the powder, it is not only made to fit the barrel tightly, but its cylindrical surface is moulded into the grooves in such a way,

that during its passage through the barrel it is constrained to turn with the grooves, and so it receives a spinning movement round its longer axis, which continues during the remainder of its flight.

5. Very few arms are accurately sighted as to *elevation;* the man, therefore, must pay attention to each shot, if it goes low or high he should report it to his Officer, who will take measures to have this defect remedied.

6. If a man suspects that his barrel is bent he should report it immediately; if there should be any dent in the barrel it will very likely burst in his hand; such defects, however, will seldom occur, except through carelessness.

7. If the trigger pulls too hard it will cause the man to alter the direction of the arm whilst firing. This is easily rectified, when necessary, by the armourer.

8. The man should pay attention, in cleaning his arms, never to rub the fore sight against any hard substance which would injure it, either forcing it to one side, or blunting it so much that he would be unable to take a proper aim.

9. If a man is to be out on service, or whenever his firelock is likely to be exposed to rain, he should stop up the nipple-hole with grease and let the cock down upon it; or if there is no grease, let him drive a peg of wood into it, and put the cap on; neither the grease nor the peg will in any way impede the action of the cap in igniting the charge, but both will disappear in the explosion.

10. If, in loading, the man observes that there is not sufficient powder in the cartridge, he should, in firing, aim a little high, as a small charge will not send so far as the regulation charge.

11. Whenever the grease round the bullet appears to be melted away, or otherwise removed from the cartridge, the sides of the bullet should be *wetted in the mouth* before putting it into the barrel—the saliva will serve the purpose of grease for the time being.

12. The necessity of always loading *standing* when practicable, and of keeping the barrel perfectly upright, should also be inculcated. When the barrel is inclined, as in loading kneeling, a great portion of the powder sticks in the fouling on the sides of the barrel, and causes difficulty in loading.

13. The Instructor should not fail to impress upon his men

the great importance of training themselves to judge distance' without which all the firing at a target is so much waste of time.

14. It has been ascertained by experiment, that if the rifled musket, pattern 1853, be fired with the elevation due to 600 yards at an object 570 yards off, the bullet will strike 2·38 feet above the mark; if the musket be fired with the same elevation at the distance of 630 yards, the bullet will strike 2·54 feet below the mark, showing that any error of 30 yards in the appreciation of distance would, at this range, cause the firer to strike the figure of a man either in the head or feet, according as the error of appreciation was under or over the correct distance.

When firing with the 300 yards' sight, the bullet will take as much as 70 yards to fall half the height of a man, owing to the trajectory of 300 yards being less curved than that of 600 yards. At 800 and 900 yards, the curve being greater that at either of the above-mentioned distances, the same fall would take place in passing over a much shorter distance, consequently the greater the distance the greater the necessity of knowing it accurately.

It is for this reason that none but well trained men should ever be allowed to fire at such distances as 800, 900, and 1,000 yards, and then only at masses of men, whose depth would make up, in some degree, for the mal-appreciation of distance. Thus, in firing at a column whose depth is 100 yards, if the man over-estimates the distance of the front rank by 100 yards, although such an error would cause him to miss the front rank, he would, if the ground is level, strike the column in its rear.

As the man, however well trained, cannot always be certain of his distance, it is preferable, when doubtful, to give the first shot an elevation rather *under* than over the correct one; the shot will then strike the ground before reaching the object, and may possibly hit "*en ricochet.*" He should be taught to watch the effect of his shot, which may generally be ascertained by observing where the bullet strikes the ground; he can then adjust his sliding-bar by raising it higher or lower, according as his first shot strikes before or beyond the object.

15. As muskets are apt to miss fire the first time, if not properly clean, great care should be taken to see that the nipple is perfectly clear before loading, by blowing down the barrel, at

the same time placing the finger over the nipple, to feel if the air passes freely through it, and afterwards by snapping a cap off, to dry up any oil or moisture that may be in the barrel.

16. If the musket frequently misses fire, it may occur from the communication-hole, by which the explosion of the cap communicates with the charge, not being of sufficient size. It may also be caused by the screw of the nipple being too long when screwed down, thereby shutting up a part of the communication-hole, and thus preventing the powder from getting into the chamber.

Preliminary Instructions in Firing.

Target Drill.

1. In this drill the man will acquire a knowledge of the use of the sights, and his progress in this branch will be tested by making him aim at different distances by means of a *rest*. The Instructor will first explain the principles of aligning the sights of a musket on an object, confining the attention of the men to the following simple rules:—

1st.—That the sights should not incline to the right or left.

2nd.—That the line of sight should be taken along the centre of the notch of the back sight and the top of the fore sight, which should cover the middle of the mark aimed at.

3rd.—That the eye should be fixed steadfastly on the mark aimed at, and not on the barrel or fore sight, which latter will be easily brought into the alignment, if the eye is fixed as directed. Particular attention must be paid to this rule, for beginners are apt to fix the eye on the fore sight instead of the mark, in which case the latter can never be distinctly seen, and the difficulty of aiming is greatly increased.

4th.—That in aiming, the left eye should be closed; if any of the men are not able to do so at first, they will soon succeed by tying a handkerchief over the left eye.

2. The instructor will then explain the difference between *fine* and *full* sight in aiming; the former being when the line of sight is taken along the bottom of the notch of the back sight, the fine point

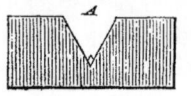

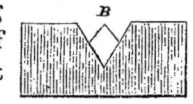

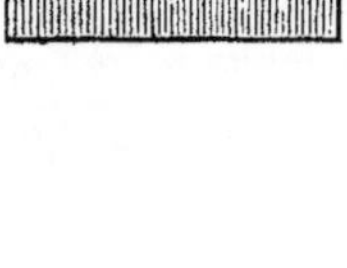

of the fore sight being only seen in the alignment as *A*; the latter is when the point of the fore sight is taken in alignment with the shoulder of the notch of the back sight, as *B*.

3. As these two methods of aiming cause a slight difference in the angle of elevation, it is necessary the man should understand that the ordinary rules for aiming are intended to apply to *half sight*, which means that the alignment is taken with the summit of the fore sight at half distance between the shoulder and bottom of the back-sight, as *C*.

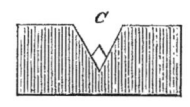

4. Having explained the foregoing rules, the Instructor will cause each man to take aim at an object of the same size as the bull's-eye used in practice, at every distance of 50 yards, from 100 to 900 yards.

5. After each man aims he will step aside, in order that the Instructor may examine and see if the aim is correctly taken. Should he observe any error, he will cause the next man to advance and point out the defect; the error, however, is always to be corrected by the man who has aimed.

Target Practice.

6. When the Party or Section has loaded by word of command, and everything is ready to commence, the Instructor will order the right hand man of the front rank to go on. After he has fired he will immediately fall three paces to the rear, having previously come to the "shoulder" from the "capping position;" the next man of the front rank will then move to the firing point and fire, after which he will also fall three paces to the rear of the point he previously occupied. In like manner, every man of the front rank will fire in succession. After which, the rear rank will commence on the right, and after firing, they will form in rear of the front rank, so that by the time the whole Section has fired one round it will have re-formed three paces in rear of its original position.

7. The Instructor will then advance his section three paces, and load, after which the firing will proceed as before.

NOTE.—The Instructor will take care not to correct a man at the moment he is firing, which would produce no other effect than to distract his attention from the object he is aiming at; but will observe attentively the position of each man, and correct him after he has fired.

DIRECTIONS FOR PRESERVING AND CLEANING THE ENFIELD RIFLE MUSKETS.

(Pattern, 1853.)

1. Placing arms forcibly in a rack, piling them carelessly (in consequence of which they often fall down), will frequently "set or crook" the barrel, more particularly at the nose, where it is thinnest, and this being the point of delivery, the arm becomes irreparably injured.

2. No musket is, on any account whatever, to be used for carrying any weight, or for any purpose for which it is not intended, as the barrel is bent very easily, and though the injury be so slight as not to be perceptible to any but a practised eye, it may be sufficient to destroy the accuracy of its shooting.

3. Great care should be taken when skirmishing not to run the muzzle of the barrel into the ground, and any person accidentally doing so, should immediately fall out; as if the piece were fired, the obstruction in the muzzle would be liable to burst the barrel. If not loaded, the dirt should be carefully removed and the barrel wiped out, for if rammed down with a charge it would tear the barrel and destroy the surface of the bore.

4. If the interior of the barrel be allowed to become rusty, the increased resistance to the passage of the bullet will probably cause the latter to strip or pass out of the grooving, or else the wooden plug may be driven through the bullet, and the arm for the time rendered useless or dangerous.

5. The surest way of preventing rust in the barrel, is to keep the bore perfectly dry, and invariably to have the muzzle stopper in, and the cock down on the nipple so as to exclude all air.

6. If a barrel is supposed to be bent, or it is found that the cartridge rams down hard, or is very loose in the barrel, or that the trigger pulls too hard, a report should be immediately made, in order that the arm may be examined by the armourer, and the defect remedied.

7. The greatest attention must be paid to the cleanliness of the pouches in the inside, especially when loose ammunition is in the pouch; so that no dust or dirt may adhere to the greased part of the cartridge, which would cause the bullet to stick in the barrel in loading.

8. A periodical examination of arms, by the Armourer, should take place, under the supervision of Officers in charge of Companies and Detachments, in order to ascertain that there is no rust in the barrel or between the barrel and the stock.

9. The above precautions for the prevention of rust or of injury to the sight or barrel, are doubly necessary with regard to the arms of Marines afloat, which should always if possible be placed in a rack, the practice of suspending them along the beams tending to destroy their efficiency with regard to exposing the bores to the influence of wet and damp and affecting the direction of the barrel.

10. The arms should be cleaned in the following manner:—

1st.—Place the musket at full cock.

2ndly.—Pour about a quarter of a pint of clean water into the barrel; in doing this, hold the musket in the left hand in a slanting direction, keeping the muzzle a little below the elbow, with the barrel downwards, to prevent any spilt water running between the barrel and stock.

3rdly.—Put a piece of rag or tow into the jag and surround it with the same, put it into the barrel immediately the water is poured in, and rub it well up and down, forcing the water out of the barrel through the nipple vent, which repeat once.

4thly.—Wipe the barrel well out with a rag or tow until quite clean and dry, and then with a rag oiled or greased.

5thly.—Wipe out the oil or grease with a clean dry rag just before firing.

NOTE.—By this means of cleaning, it is expected there will be very little liability of the barrel becoming rusted, and seldom any necessity for removing the barrel from the stock, which is always objectionable.

NAVAL CUTLASS EXERCISE.

ENGAGE

NAVAL CUTLAS EXERCISE.

EXPLANATION

The Large Circle shows the direction of the Cuts marked Cut 1, Cut 2, Etc. The Small Circles show that the same may be delivered at the Head, Body or Leg. The principal figure shows the defensive position called "Engage" being the best for a swordsman to be prepared to Attack or Defend when opposed to the Sword, Bayonet or Pike. The four small figures show the four Guards or Parries, for either Cut or Point, & the Position from which the Points are delivered without further preparation.

NAVAL CUTLASS EXERCISE.

IN this Exercise there are only Four Cuts, Four Guards, and Two Points given from the Guards; these being all that are necessary to enable a man to become an efficient Swordsman. There are also only Three Positions; and these are taught sword in hand—the "First" being the position of "Attention," the "Second" the "Engaging," or Defensive Position, the "Third" the "Attacking Position."

A Division falls in, either in single or double files, with Swords sheathed. If with Drill Swords, without scabbards, the Swords are to be held in the left hand as if sheathed.

PREPARATORY MOVEMENTS.

ATTENTION. { Body erect; shoulders square to the front; and heels closed.

DRAW SWORDS. { At the word "Draw," grasp the hilt with the right hand, and scabbard with the left; the rear rank (if two deep) stepping back one pace at the same instant.

At "Swords," draw out smartly, and bring the fore arm horizontal, with the sword upright, the fingers and thumb encircling the hilt, being the position of "Carry Swords."

SLOPE SWORDS. { Rest the sword in a sloping position against the shoulder, by easing the grasp.

CARRY SWORDS. { Grasp, and carry the sword upright, as before.

RETURN SWORDS. { At the word "Return," grasp the scabbard with the left hand, and enter the point about one inch, glancing the eye, to direct it, for the moment.

At "Swords," return the blade home, and quit the right hand smartly, the rear rank closing up at the same instant.

The Division being in Close Files with Swords Sloped.

FROM THE RIGHT (or Left) EXTEND.
If from the right, the right file (having distance from his own right) remains steady; the rest open out in quick or double time, as may be directed; the front rank, in succession (glancing the eye over the right shoulder), extend the right arm and sword; and, when two inches clear, "halt," "front," "dress," and "slope." The rear rank move off with the front rank, and cover correctly when halted, but they are not to extend the arm.
If from the left, apply the same rule; the front rank men looking over the left shoulder, to judge the time to halt.

TAKE OPEN ORDER FOR EXERCISE.
The front rank men advance across the deck (or about eight paces), "halt," and face "right about."

PROVE DISTANCE.
Keeping the feet steady, turn the body to the right, look over the right shoulder, extend the right arm and sword, as far to the rear as possible, with the back of the hand up, then, without pausing, and keeping the eyes in the direction of the point, pass the sword round to the *left* front and back again over the shoulder to the "Slope."

ON THE RIGHT (or Left) CLOSE.
The front rank recross the deck; and both ranks turning towards the standing file, close, "halt," "front," and "dress," in succession, rear rank remaining at Open order, ready to return swords, or to extend again.

FIRST PART.

The First Part, whether Cutting, Guarding, or Pointing, is to be practised by using the right and left arms alternately whilst standing in an unconstrained attitude, either with the shoulders square to the front, or with the one shoulder inclined backward; the one position being intended for unconstrained *Training* exercise, the other for applying only such movements of the first as are necessary for the practice of Attack and Defence.

As far as practicable, the files are to stand exactly opposite each other, by way of a Target to aim at; and throughout the exercise they should look each other full in the face, in order to acquire a good aim either of Cut or Point.

The cuts "*One*" and "*Three*" are inside cuts; "*Two*" and "*Four*," outside cuts, with either arm.

THE TRAINING CUTTING EXERCISE.

The Division being at Extended Order.

TRAINING EXERCISE. } A caution.

PREPARE. { Separate the feet sideways about two lengths of the foot from heel to heel, preserving the same direct line to the front, and distance from file to file. Bring the sword to the "Carry;" place the left fore-arm square across the body, and grasp the clothing with the hand; elbows close, and shoulders square to the front.

NOTE.—The sword thus grasped is never to be shifted in the hand throughout the exercise of Cutting, Guarding, or Pointing.

CUTLASS EXERCISE.

Cuts One & Two. — A caution.

Prepare. — Raise the hand until the pommel appears level with the shoulder of the man opposite, keeping the arm bent as at the "Carry," resting the blade lightly on the sword-arm shoulder for cut "One;" and, after cutting "One," on the reverse shoulder for cut "Two."

One. — Keeping the body, legs, and feet steady, without stiffness, cut diagonally downwards from shoulder to hip twice over, *inside* and *outside* alternately, extending the arm, with the pommel leading, and (in drill time, counting 1—2—3—4,) deliver each cut with a full, unconstrained sweep of the arm, re-bending it after each cut, and prepare to repeat the same.

Proof. — Each man in succession, or two men at a time, under the particular notice of the Instructor, to repeat these cuts, in order to prove that each understands the instruction, and to allow a timely rest to the class.

NOTE.—The Instructor, with sword in hand, will ensure correctness better by occasionally showing the movements himself, than by giving any detail, however explicit.

One. — Repeat the same cuts, correcting errors as may have been pointed out.

Carry Swords. — As before, to ensure the proper grasp, ready for the following cuts.

Change Arms. — Reverse the position of the arms, by bringing the sword to the "Carry" in the left hand.

NOTE.—By the same words of command practise the foregoing exercise, and then replace the sword in the right hand, and so on throughout, on Changing arms

CUTLASS EXERCISE.

Cuts Three and Four. { A caution.

Prepare. { Raise the arm, and prepare exactly as for the cuts "One" and "Two."

Three. { Cut horizontally from shoulder to shoulder, inside and outside alternately, in the same manner as cutting "One" and "Two."

Note.—Prove and repeat the same as above, "Carry swords," and "Change arms."

The Four Cuts. { A caution.

Prepare. { Prepare to cut "One" as before, ready to combine the cuts, at the word "Assault."

Assault. { Deliver the cuts "One" and "Two" downwards, and "Three" and "Four" straight across, in the time of 1—2—3—4.

Note.—Prove and repeat the same, "Carry swords," and "Change arms." With a Class under instruction for the first time, the Instructor is to prove each man separately at the "Assault," pointing out and correcting errors; particularly that of checking the sweep of the cut too soon by the quick turn of the wrist, thereby exercising the wrist only instead of the whole arm, and thus hitting with the flat of the blade, an error as readily detected by the ear as by the eye, causing a noise in the air, the reverse of the short whistling sound which proves the true leading of the edge.

After the Instructor has proved that each man can deliver the four cuts together in drill time, the whole may occasionally be ordered to deliver them as quickly as possible at the word "Assault," each judging his own time.

Slope Swords. { Close the heels, replace the left arm by the side, and "Slope," coming to the position of "Attention."

The Four Cuts.
Standing in an attitude of Attack and Defence.

PERFORM SWORD EXERCISE.
> Raise the arm smartly, and prepare for cut "One;" at the same instant point the right foot direct to the front, and quickly place the left foot behind the right, at right angles with it, and the left fore-arm behind the back, with the hand closed. The space between the feet to be about two lengths of each person's own foot from heel to heel, the knees to be slightly bent, and the weight of the body to rest equally on both legs.

THE CUTS. — A caution.

ONE. — Cut inside from shoulder to hip, and prepare to cut "Two."

TWO. — Cut outside from shoulder to hip, and prepare to cut "Three."

THREE. — Cut inside from shoulder to shoulder, and prepare to cut "Four."

FOUR. — Cut outside from shoulder to shoulder, and prepare to cut "One" again.

NOTE.—The Cuts are now to be combined as before at the word "Assault;" but with a Class for the first time, the Instructor should name *the part* to be aimed at.

THE HEAD, BODY, OR LEG. — A caution.

ASSAULT. — Deliver the four cuts high or low, as directed, and prepare to repeat the same.

SLOPE SWORDS. — Close the left foot smartly to the right, and "Slope" as before.

CHANGE ARMS. — Place the sword in the left hand at the "Slope."

NOTE.—Repeat the same exercise, and after Sloping swords replace the sword in the right hand.

THE TRAINING GUARDING EXERCISE.

The position of the arm when at the "Carry," with respect to the grasp of the hand; the natural firm position of the wrist; the angle or bend of the arm at the elbow, as well as the angle the sword forms with the fore-arm; and the distance the hand is then from the vertical line of the body, viz., the length of the fore-arm, are particular points to be kept in view in teaching the formation of the Guards.

The *First* and *Fourth* are inside guards; the *Second* and *Third* outside guards.

TRAINING EXERCISE. { A caution.

PREPARE. { As before, feet separated sideways, and sword at the "Carry."

FIRST. { Raise the arm smartly, carrying the hand straight up as high as the crown of the head (elbow still bent as at the "Carry"), drop the point, and incline the edge upwards to the front.

NOTE.—This guard defends every part within the sword arm, from the crown of the head to the leg, by raising or lowering the arm as necessary; but in this position it will suffice to have it formed well and quickly as above, to insure which the Instructor must repeat the words "Carry swords," and "First;" as often as necessary.

CARRY SWORDS. { As before.

SECOND. { Square the upper arm smartly with the shoulder, the fore-arm to be in a front line with and a little below the elbow, the point inclined to the front, and the edge to the right.

CARRY SWORDS. { As before.

NOTE.—This guard defends the right side from the armpit to the leg, by raising or lowering the arm. Before proceeding with the *Third* guard the Instructor must repeat the words of command—"First," "Second"—with life, until the whole move the sword and arm smartly *up* and *down*, striking and parrying, as if it were with the hilt of the sword, from the one guard to the other; being careful to keep the point below the hilt in both cases, so that the one guard position, when at rest, may be parallel with the other.

G 2

THIRD. { Carry the hilt midway between the shoulder and elbow, directing the edge to the right front, the upper arm to be quite close at the armpit, having the fore-arm thus firmly stayed out from the body. The blade with the point raised, and bearing away to the left front.

CARRY SWORDS. { As before.

NOTE.—This guard defends the head from a vertical cut, and the sword arm, right breast, shoulder, and cheek from the *outside* cuts, by raising or lowering the arm; the words of command—"Second," "Third"—to be repeated until correctly formed, and then "First," "Second," "Third."

FOURTH. { Carry the arm well across the body, the upper part at the armpit quite close, the hand well off to the left front, having the fore-arm thus firmly stayed out. The blade with the point raised, and bearing away to the right front.

CARRY SWORDS. { As before.

NOTE.—This guard defends the head from a vertical cut, and the sword arm, left breast, shoulder, and cheek from the *inside* cuts, by raising or lowering the arm; the words "Third" and "Fourth" to be repeated, when the hand is to pass quickly from right to left and left to right, parrying as though with the hilt only, being careful that the blade covers the head at each movement; then repeat the words of command, "First," "Second," "Third," "Fourth," until the class are prepared to combine the guards by the word "Defend."

DEFEND. { Combine the four guards, keeping the same time, as in the four cuts, smartly moving from guard to guard.

CARRY SWORDS.—CHANGE ARMS.

NOTE.—Practise the foregoing guards, and then replace the sword in the right hand.

PROOF. { Each man separately to form the four guards under the particular notice of the Instructor, who will be careful that each man looks direct to the front, and moves the arm smartly from guard to guard.

NOTE.—After having proved that each man understands the guards, the whole should be ordered to form them as quickly as possible at the word "Defend."

CARRY SWORDS.—SLOPE SWORDS.

The Four Guards
(Added to the Four Cuts).
Standing in an Attitude of Attack and Defence.

PERFORM SWORD EXERCISE. } As before.

NOTE.—Repeat the words of command for the Cuts, as under.

THE CUTS. "One"—"Two"—"Three"—"Four."

THE GUARDS. } A caution.

FIRST. { Defend the head with the First Guard high.

SECOND. { Defend the right side with the Second Guard high.

THIRD. { Defend the sword arm and shoulder from the *outside* cuts.

FOURTH. { Defend the sword arm and breast from the *inside* cuts.

NOTE.—The Guards are now to be combined, as before, at the word "Defend;" but with a Class for the first time, the Instructor should name the *particular part* to be defended.

THE HEAD, BODY, OR LEG. } A caution.

DEFEND. { Form the four guards in succession, high or low, as directed; counting 1—2—3—4 for the *head* or *body*, and 1—2 for the *leg;* the *First* and *Second* low guards alone defend the leg.

SLOPE SWORDS. } As before.

CHANGE ARMS. } As before.

NOTE.—Repeat the same exercise, and again replace the sword in the right hand.

THE TRAINING POINTING EXERCISE.

Too much attention cannot be paid by the Instructor in teaching the Pointing Practice; as the Point, if properly directed, can always be delivered, in close quarters, where the Cut cannot, and at all times much quicker.

The Point is to be given instantly and direct from any one of the four Guards at the breast of the man opposite, without shifting the grasp, drawing back or lowering the arm.

Either of the four Guards is a Parry or Defence (*up* or *down*, *right* or *left*, according to the Attack), against the point of Sword, Bayonet, or Pike, and from which an instantaneous return of Cut or Thrust can be delivered.

TRAINING EXERCISE.	A caution.
PREPARE.	As before.
FIRST.	Form First Guard.
POINT.	In one quick motion direct the point to the front by extending the arm, the hand moving in a straight line to the front of the First Guard position and without altering the direction of the edge, ready to Parry or Guard again.
FIRST.	Brace up the arm quickly and Parry *upwards*, by forming First Guard as before.
POINT AND DEFEND.	A caution.
ONE.	Deliver the same point, and Parry with *First* Guard, twice over, as quickly as possible.
CARRY SWORDS.	As before.
CHANGE ARMS.	As before.

NOTE.—Repeat the above, and then replace the sword in the right hand, and so on throughout.

SECOND.	{	Form Second Guard.
POINT.	{	Direct the point quickly at the breast, as from the First Guard.
SECOND.	{	Brace up the arm quickly and Parry *downwards* by forming Second Guard, as before.
POINT AND DEFEND.	{	A caution.
TWO.	{	Deliver the same point, and Parry with *Second* Guard twice over quickly.
CARRY SWORDS.	{	As before.
THIRD.	{	Form Third Guard.
POINT.	{	Direct the point as from the Second Guard.
THIRD.	{	Brace up the arm quickly, and Parry to the *right* by forming Third Guard.
POINT AND DEFEND.	{	A caution.
THREE.	{	Deliver the same point, and Parry with *Third* Guard, twice over quickly.
CARRY SWORDS.	{	As before.
FOURTH.	{	Form Fourth Guard.
POINT.	{	Direct the point at the breast, by quickly extending the arm, the hand moving in a straight line to the front of the Fourth Guard position, and without altering the direction of the edge.
FOURTH.	{	Brace up the arm quickly, and Parry to the *left*, by forming Fourth Guard.

POINT AND DEFEND. { A caution.

FOUR. { Deliver the same point, and Parry with *Fourth* Guard, twice over quickly.

CARRY SWORDS. { As before.

NOTE.—The points delivered from the *First*, *Second*, and *Third* guards are literally one, being delivered with the back of the hand up. That delivered from the *Fourth* guard, with the palm of the hand up, is the other, and the two should now be practised and combined together as follows :—

FOURTH. { As before, form Fourth Guard.

POINT. { As before.

THIRD. { As before, form Third Guard.

POINT. { As before.

FIRST. { As before, form First Guard.

NOTE.—To prepare the Class to repeat or to combine the above four motions of Pointing and Parrying, and before commencing to prove the men individually, the Instructor should give the word of command—" Point and Defend," as a caution.

POINT AND DEFEND. { Form Fourth Guard, ready to point from it.

POINT. { Point from *Fourth* Guard, then form *Third* Guard; point from *Third* Guard, then form *First* Guard; counting 1—2—3—4.

CARRY SWORDS. { As before.

PROOF. { Each man singly, commencing from the Fourth Guard, to repeat the Pointing and Parrying in four motions, under the particular notice of the Instructor.

NOTE.—After the Instructor has proved the Class, the whole should be ordered to "Point and Defend" as quickly as possible, by the one word of command, "Point," with right and left arm alternately.

CARRY SWORDS.—CHANGE ARMS.

The Two Points

(Added to the Cuts and Guards).

Standing in an Attitude of Attack and Defence.

PERFORM SWORD EXERCISE. — As before.

NOTE.—Repeat the words of command for the Cuts and Guards, as under.

THE CUTS. — "One"—"Two"—"Three"—"Four."

THE GUARDS. — "First"—"Second"—"Third"—"Fourth."

THE POINTS. — A caution.

POINT. — From Fourth Guard, and keep the arm extended.

THIRD. — Form Third Guard.

POINT. — From Third Guard, arm extended.

FIRST. — Form First Guard.

POINT AND DEFEND. — Form Fourth Guard.

POINT. — Repeat the above four movements, counting 1—2—3—4.

SLOPE SWORDS. — As before.

CHANGE ARMS. — As before.

NOTE.—Repeat the above exercise, and after Sloping swords, again replace the sword in the right hand.

THE TRAINING COMBINATION EXERCISE.

The Cuts, as well as the Points, are now to be delivered direct from a Defensive position, care being taken not to raise the arm higher, or draw it back further than the Guard position; the whole being an exercise preparatory for the quick return Cuts and Points of the Attack and Defence.

TRAINING EXERCISE. { A caution.

PREPARE. { As before.

FIRST. { Form First Guard ready to cut "One."

CUT ONE. { Deliver the cut "One" direct from the First Guard, recovering the sword to the Fourth Guard.

POINT. { Point smartly from Fourth Guard, but instantly (without a pause) withdraw the arm and sword to the same guard, ready to cut or point again.

NOTE.—The word "Point" to be repeated once or twice at first, to ensure correctness.

CUT TWO. { Deliver the cut "Two" direct from the Fourth Guard, and recover the sword to the Third Guard.

POINT. { Point smartly from the Third Guard, but instantly withdraw to the same guard.

CUT THREE. { Deliver the cut "Three," recovering the sword to the Fourth Guard.

POINT. { As before.

CUT FOUR. { Deliver the cut "Four," and recover the sword to the First Guard.

POINT. { Point smartly from the First Guard, but instantly withdraw to the First Guard, ready to repeat the same, or to combine the whole by one word of command.

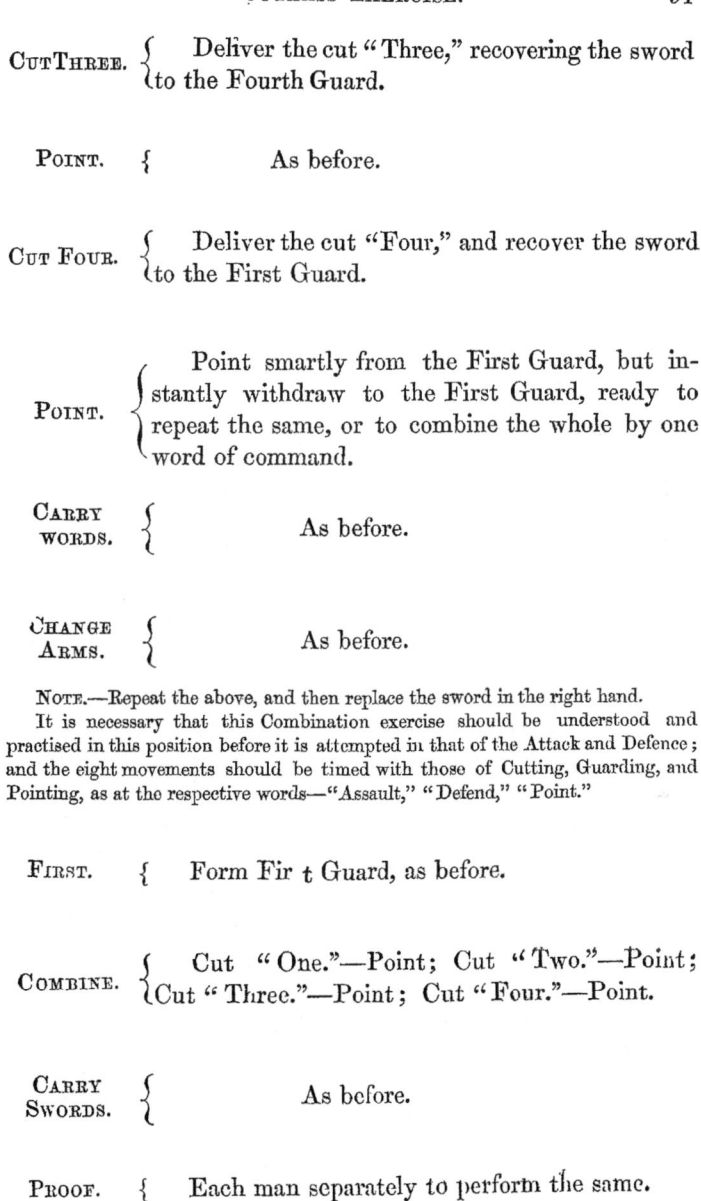

CARRY SWORDS. { As before.

CHANGE ARMS. { As before.

NOTE.—Repeat the above, and then replace the sword in the right hand.

It is necessary that this Combination exercise should be understood and practised in this position before it is attempted in that of the Attack and Defence; and the eight movements should be timed with those of Cutting, Guarding, and Pointing, as at the respective words—"Assault," "Defend," "Point."

FIRST. { Form First Guard, as before.

COMBINE. { Cut "One."—Point; Cut "Two."—Point; Cut "Three."—Point; Cut "Four."—Point.

CARRY SWORDS. { As before.

PROOF. { Each man separately to perform the same.

SLOPE SWORDS. { As before.

The Combination
(Added to the Cuts, Guards, and Points).
Standing in an Attitude of Attack and Defence.

Perform Sword Exercise. { As before.

Note.—Repeat the words of command for the Cuts, Guards, and Points, as under.

The Cuts. "One"—"Two"—"Three"—"Four."

The Guards. "First"—"Second"—"Third"—"Fourth."

The Points. "Point"—"Third." "Point"—"First."

The Combination. { A caution.

Cut One. { Step smartly forward one short space with the right foot (its own length at least), keep the left foot firm, the body upright, and straighten the left knee; at the same instant deliver the cut "One" from the First Guard, and form Fourth Guard; the arm and foot moving together.

Point. { Keeping the body and feet steady, give point; then instantly step back again, withdrawing the arm and sword to the Fourth Guard (arm and foot moving together).

Cut Two. { Step forward as before, and cut "Two," and form Third Guard.

Point. { As before, Point and step back to the Third Guard.

Cut Three. { Step forward, cut "Three," and form Fourth Guard.

Point. { Point, and step back to the Fourth Guard.

CUT FOUR.	{	Step forward, cut "Four," and form First Guard.
POINT.	{	Point and step back to the First Guard; thus ready to repeat the same.
COMBINE.	{	Combine the foregoing eight motions, in drill time, as at the respective words, "Assault," "Defend," "Point."
SLOPE SWORDS.	{	As before.
CHANGE ARMS.	{	As before.

NOTE.—Repeat the above exercise, and after Sloping swords replace the sword in the right hand.

At this stage of the Exercise, such men as are likely to become Instructors should occasionally be formed into small Classes to practise drilling one another in turns; but the *Training Exercise* should not then be gone through. It will suffice to go through the Cuts, Guards, and Points, word by word, and movement by movement, as below; the Class changing arms, as each man takes his turn, so as to make the most of the time without fatiguing one another. The man drilling should see that all are right, and correct any individual error before he gives the next word; for instance, he must see that the preparation for each Cut is correct; that the Guards are properly formed; the Points well delivered; and, particularly, that the Combination is performed with life.

CLASS PRACTICE.

The Class being at Extended Order for Exercise.

	The Cuts.	The Guards.	The Points.	The Combination.	
PERFORM SWORD EXERCISE.	ONE. TWO. THREE. FOUR.	FIRST. SECOND. THIRD. FOURTH.	POINT. THIRD. POINT. FIRST.	CUT ONE. POINT. CUT TWO. POINT. CUT THREE. POINT. CUT FOUR. POINT.	SLOPE SWORDS.

INSPECTION EXERCISE.

The Division being in Single or Double Files, with Swords sheathed.

ATTENTION. { Body erect, shoulders square to the front, and heels closed.

DRAW SWORDS. { Draw, and "Carry" swords. Rear rank stepping back one pace.

SLOPE SWORDS. { On shoulder, fore-arm horizontal.

FROM THE RIGHT (or Left) EXTEND. { Open out to sword and arm's length. Rear rank covering the front.

TAKE OPEN ORDER FOR EXERCISE. { Front rank cross the deck, and face "right about."

PROVE DISTANCE. { All round, from right rear, to left front.

INSPECTION EXERCISE. { A caution.

PERFORM SWORD EXERCISE. { Prepare to cut "One," left foot and arm to the rear.

ASSAULT. { Cut "One" and "Two" diagonally downward, and "Three" and "Four" straight across.

DEFEND. { Defend the *head, right side, sword arm,* and *breast* in succession.

POINT. { Point from Fourth Guard, form Third Guard; point from Third Guard, form First Guard.

COMBINE. { Cut "One."—Point; Cut "Two."—Point; Cut "Three."—Point; Cut "Four."—Point.

SLOPE SWORDS. { As before.

NOTE.—Here may follow, if necessary, the Inspection Exercise of the Attack and Defence. *See* page 106.

ON THE RIGHT CLOSE.	Close to the right. Rear rank at *Open* order.
CARRY SWORDS.	Upright in the hand.
RETURN SWORDS.	Return. Rear rank taking *Close* order.

The above is a brief summary of the Cutlass Exercise, being all that is necessary at any General Inspection. It may also be performed from the position of "Attention," by the one word of command, "Perform Sword Exercise;" when timing the motions, they "Assault," "Defend," "Point," "Combine," and "Slope" together.

To test the force, efficacy, and precision of the Sword Cut, the men should occasionally be permitted to compete with each other, by cutting with a Service Cutlass at triangular pieces of lead about eight inches long and one or two inches wide. The lead may either be suspended, or placed standing on one end.

To enable them to do so effectually, as well as to teach them the right method of proving distance at the Attack and Defence Practices, they should be made acquainted with the strong and weak parts of the sword, called the Forte and Feeble; the *Forte* being the one-third of the blade nearest the hilt, to be used for the Defence generally; the *Feeble*, the one-third nearest the point, to be used for the Attack. But the precise spot, or Centre of Percussion, in which the whole force of the blow is concentrated, will readily be found by holding the sword lightly, and letting the blade fall by its own weight, either on its back or edge, on any hard substance; if it fall on any other spot than that sought, the blade will jar or vibrate, but if at that spot, it will remain at rest. *See* Diagram.

SECOND PART.

THE ATTACK AND DEFENCE.

THE following System of Attack and Defence is based on that adopted by the best practical Swordsmen, when at independent hand-to-hand encounters. The main object throughout being to train men for actual conflict in as short a time as possible. The Attack and Defence Practices are purposely composed of but few movements, which, by repetition at each succeeding drill, cannot fail to train the *eye to be quick*, and the *hand to be ready* for any emergency.

There are Three Practices:—one Cutting and Guarding, one Pointing and Guarding, and a Combination of both, consisting of Four sections of three movements each, and performed, when completed, by the same simple words of command, "One," "Two," "Three," "Four;" but at the *first time*, and on *all training occasions* each section should be practised separately, as hereafter detailed.

For Cutting and Guarding, four points of attack, viz., *Head* (*one*), *Arm* (*two*), *Thigh* (*three*), *Leg* (*four*), and two cuts, need only be borne in mind; the diagonal cut "One," *inside*, at head and thigh, and cut "Two," *outside*, at arm and leg.

For Pointing and Guarding, the words "One," "Two," &c., at once denote the Guard to Point and Parry from; and the Combination Practice is simply substituting a Point for a Cut in the Practice.

ATTACK AND DEFENCE.

The Division being at Extended Order for Exercise.

PREPARE FOR ATTACK AND DEFENCE. { Either rank advance on the other, or both ranks may advance towards each other, and "halt" and "dress" at the distance of *two* ordinary paces apart. If at *Close* order, to extend, and take up the same position.

THE ENGAGING GUARD.

NOTE.—Any one of the four guards may be taken as an *Engaging* or *preparatory* guard for Attack and Defence, by straightening or relieving the sword arm from its braced up guard position, care being had not to show an opening *above*, and *below*, or *inside* and *outside* of the blade at the same time.

The *Second* Guard, however, being the best for a *broad swordsman* to be prepared to attack or defend from, when opposed to the sword, pike, or bayonet, is to be generally adopted.

ENGAGE. { Step back smartly to the position of "Perform Sword Exercise," and form *Second* Guard, raising the arm fully as high as the shoulder, and keeping it loose and free, with the elbow slightly bent; hilt in line with and covering the elbow, and the point inclined to the front, the right side being thus covered from a direct cut or point.

REST. { Keeping the feet steady, lower the sword arm, and "stand easy."

NOTE.—This word of command to be given throughout the Practices, whenever any explanation or correction of errors is necessary.

ENGAGE. { As before.

SLOPE SWORDS. { Spring smartly up to the position of "Attention."

NOTE.—The words "Engage" and "Slope Swords" to be repeated until done smartly.

The Cutting and Guarding Practice, as shown in the arrangement of the Practices at page 106, will be readily understood by the following detail of the *Second* Section.

H

FIRST PRACTICE.

Cutting and Guarding.

Front Rank or Right Files.	Rear Rank or Left Files.
SEC. 2ND. HEAD, ARM, HEAD.	
ENGAGE.	

SEC. 2ND.
HEAD, ARM, { A caution.
HEAD.

ENGAGE. { As before.

HEAD.
| Step smartly forward one short pace with the right foot, and cut "*One*" at the head, in the direction of the face, and remain out, ready to meet the *return*. | Keep the feet firm, and defend the head by the First Guard, ready to return. |

Swords joined at forte and feeble.

NOTE.—The attacking file, if necessary, is now to correct his measure, by moving forward or backward, so as to prove his own distance.

ARM.
| Remaining steady with feet and body, *defend* the arm by the Third Guard. | Remaining steady, *return* cut "Two" at the arm, in the direction of the face. |

Swords joined lightly.

HEAD. { Return the cut, as before. | Defend the head, as before.

Swords joined.

ENGAGE or SLOPE SWORDS.

NOTE.—To Slope swords from the *lunge;* first replace the right foot as at the word "Engage," and then close the feet as before.

Repeat the above until understood; the same three movements are next to be *completed* at one word of command, when each party of two, doing their best, judge their own time; it is, however, to be understood that although the cuts are to be given with life, they are not to be given with determined full force, for a well exercised arm can hardly avoid cutting heavily without the determination to do so.

ATTACK AND DEFENCE.

	Right Files.	Left Files.
JUDGING THE TIME. HEAD, ARM, HEAD.	A caution.	
TWO.	Step out, *attack* the head, *defend* the arm, and *return* at the head.	Remain steady, *defend* the head, *return* at the arm, and again *defend* the head.

Swords joined.

NOTE.—Repeat the same twice at least, and then reverse the practice by the Left files commencing, and so on throughout the whole of the sections, giving the caution *Right* or *Left Files*, to prevent both attacking at the same time.

THE RALLYING PRACTICE.

NOTE.—At this stage of the drill, it will be good practice to enliven the men, as well as to accustom them to measure the proper distance for actual encounters, to separate the ranks six or eight paces apart, and to direct the one rank to run towards the other, and have a short rally in their own time; simply to *attack*, *defend*, and *return* once, according to a given caution, and then to retire smartly to their former position, ready to repeat the same, or to meet the attack.

RALLYING PRACTICE.	A caution.	
FILES ABOUT.	The ranks separate across the deck, and face each other; all standing with swords lowered, or at *Rest*.	

NOTE.—The Instructor may here give any change in the cautionary words of command of the Cutting and Guarding Practice at pleasure, such as Head, Head, Thigh, or Arm, Head, Head.

HEAD, HEAD, ARM.	A caution.	
MARCH or DOUBLE.	Advance, and when in measure, *attack*, *defend*, and *return* (according to the caution), and then retire back.	Keeping the sword lowered until the moment of attack, step back with left foot, *defend*, *return*, and *defend*, and again "stand easy" as soon as the right file retires.

NOTE.—The moment the Instructor perceives any misunderstanding, he is to call the men to attention, by the word of command "Halt;" when every man is to *fall in*, in his own rank immediately. Having practised both ranks alike, they are to be closed again.

SECOND PRACTICE.

Pointing and Guarding.

Right Files.	Left Files.
(Sec. 1st. Point & First Guard.) A caution.	
Engage. As before.	
Point. Step forward, and point direct at the breast, keeping the direction of the edge as at the "Engage;" the arm extended and free, with the sword bearing lightly, ready to defend a return cut, or point.	Remaining steady, parry *upwards* by First Guard, ready to return a cut or point.

NOTE.—As in the first movement of the Cutting and Guarding Practice, so here, the attacking file is to measure his own pointing distance, which should not be so close by *four* inches at least.

Point. Remaining steady, parry *upwards* by First Guard, timely seizing the feeble of opponent's blade, being careful not to lower the arm. Both files thus reversing the position of the swords, ready to repeat the same.	Remaining steady, return a point direct at the breast, by quickly extending the arm without lowering it.

ATTACK AND DEFENCE.

	Right Files.	Left Files.
Point.	Return the same point.	Defend by First Guard, as before.

Note.—Repeat the same, movement by movement, till well understood; for too much attention cannot be paid to this Point and Parry Practice, as it should always be borne in mind that a well-directed Point is given much quicker, and is much more likely to disable an opponent than a Cut, which is seldom fatal unless given by a powerful and good swordsman.

The Instructor should have a practical knowledge of this part of the exercise, and where men for the first time misunderstand his verbal instructions, he must, with sword in hand, stand in front of, and show them himself.

The three movements are next to be combined, as under.

Judging the Time. Point & First Guard.	A caution.
Engage.	As before.
One.	Lunge and *point*, *defend*, and *return* the same, and remain out, with the arm extended.	Standing steady, defend by First Guard, *return* at once, and again *defend* by First Guard.

Swords joined lightly.

Engage, or Slope Swords.

Note.—Repeat the same as often as necessary, and reverse the practice.

Sec. 2nd. Point & Second Guard.	A caution.

Note.—In this Section, when thus detailed, both files will be cautioned to show an opening under the sword.

Engage.	As before.

	Right Files.	*Left Files.*
First.	Look under the sword, or apply the First Guard as an Engaging guard, with the arm nearly straight, but loose and free.	
Point.	Lunge and point direct at the breast.	Defend, or parry *downwards* by Second Guard.
Point.	Defend by Second Guard.	Return the point *under*, but at breast.
Point.	Return the same.	Defend by Second Guard again.

Swords joined lightly after each point.

Engage or Slope Swords.

Sec. 3rd. Point & Third Guard.	A caution.	
Engage.	As before.	
Point.	Lunge and point as before.	Defend, or parry to the *right* by Third Guard.
Point.	Defend by Third Guard.	Return, *over* the sword, at the breast.
Point.	Return at the breast from Third Guard.	Defend by Third Guard.

Swords joined lightly after each point.

Engage, or Slope Swords.

ATTACK AND DEFENCE.

Right Files.	Left Files.

SEC. 4TH.
POINT & FOURTH GUARD. { A caution.

NOTE.—In this Section, when thus detailed, both files will be cautioned to give an opening for the practice of Pointing and Parrying from the Fourth guard.

ENGAGE. { As before.

THIRD. { Both files to apply the *Third* as an Engaging guard: but with the arm nearly straight, and the point lowered to the front, just clear of joining blades.

	Right Files.	Left Files.
POINT.	Lunge and point *inside*, the edge directed as at the Third Guard.	Defend, or parry to the *left*, by Fourth Guard.
POINT.	Defend or parry by Fourth Guard.	Return the point *inside* from Fourth Guard.
POINT.	Return from Fourth Guard.	Defend again by Fourth Guard.

Swords joined lightly after each point.

ENGAGE, or SLOPE SWORDS.

NOTE.—Practise the Second, Third, and Fourth Sections, "Judging the time" at the respective words of command—*Two—Three—Four*—in the same manner as the First Section.

THIRD PRACTICE.

The Combination of Cutting, Guarding, and Pointing.

This being simply a Combination of the two foregoing practices, will be readily understood by only detailing the *Second* and *Third* Sections, as follows. The four Sections are then to be practised—" Judging the time "—at the respective words of command, *One—Two—Three—Four.*

	Right Files.	*Left Files.*
Sec. 2nd. Head, Arm, Point.	A caution.	
Engage.	As before.	
Head.	Lunge, and attack the head.	Remain, and defend the head.
Arm.	Defend the arm by Third Guard.	Return cut "Two" at the arm.
Point & First Guard.	A caution.	
Point.	Return a point at the breast.	Defend by First Guard.

Swords lightly joined.

Engage or Slope Swords.

ATTACK AND DEFENCE.

	Right Files.	Left Files.
Sec. 3rd. Head, Thigh, Point.	A caution.	
Engage.	As before.	
Head.	Lunge and attack the head.	Remain, and defend the head.
Thigh.	Defend the thigh by low First Guard.	Return cut "One" at the thigh.
Point & Second Guard.	A caution.	
Point.	Return a point, on receiving an opening *under* the sword.	First give an opening, by raising the sword arm, as though to defend the head, then parry by Second Guard.

Swords lightly joined.

Engage or Slope Swords.

As an Inspection Exercise, the following words of command and movements need only be repeated once, the right and left files lunging and recovering alternately. At the word of command, "*One*," the Right files *lunge, attack, defend,* and *return*, as directed by the cautionary words, "Head—Head—Head," or "Point and First Guard," or "Head—Head—Point;" the left files standing, *defend, return,* and *defend,* swords joined at *forte* and *feeble*. At the next word, "*Two*," the Left files will lunge, and attack as the right files are recovering; and so on, alternately, completing three movements.

In the tabular arrangement of the practices, the Cuts are denoted by the words, *One, Two,* &c.; the Guards by *First, Second,* &c.; and the Points as delivered, *Over, Under, Inside,* or *Outside* of the opponent's sword, according to the opening at the moment of attack.

When men are practising at drilling one another in turns, (*see* page 93), they should only go through the Attack and Defence Practices, as above explained, and should then use *sticks and handguards,* if available, so as not to fatigue one another unnecessarily.

ATTACK AND DEFENCE.

The Division being prepared for Attack and Defence.

Words of Command.		Front Rank or Right Files.			Rear Rank or Left Files.		
Cautionary.	Executive.	Cut, Guard, or Point.	Cut, Guard, or Point.	Cut, Guard, or Point.	Cut, Guard, or Point.	Cut, Guard, or Point.	Cut, Guard, or Point.
FIRST PRACTICE. *(Cuts and Guards.)*	*Engage.*						
Head, Head, Head.	*One.*	One.	First.	One.	First.	One.	First.
Head, Arm, Head.	*Two.*	First.	Two.	First.	One.	Third.	One.
Head, Thigh, Head.	*Three.*	One.	First.	One.	First.	One.	First.
Head, Leg, Head.	*Four.*	First.	Two.	First.	One.	Second.	One.
Slope	*Swords.*						
SECOND PRACTICE. *(Points and Guards.)*	*Engage.*						
Point & First Guard.	*One.*	Over.	First.	Under.	First.	Under.	First.
Point & Second Guard.	*Two.*	Second.	Under.	Second.	Under.	Second.	Under.
Point & Third Guard.	*Three.*	Over.	Third.	Outside.	Third.	Outside.	Third.
Point & Fourth Guard.	*Four.*	Fourth.	Inside.	Fourth.	Inside.	Fourth.	Inside.
Slope	*Swords.*						
THIRD PRACTICE. *(The Combination.)*	*Engage.*						
Head, Head, Point.	*One.*	One.	First.	Under.	First.	One.	Second.
Head, Arm, Point.	*Two.*	First.	Two.	First.	One.	Third.	Over.
Head, Thigh, Point.	*Three.*	One.	First.	Under.	First.	One.	Second.
Head, Leg, Point.	*Four.*	First.	Two.	First.	One.	Second.	Over.
Slope	*Swords.*						

The above arrangement shows at a glance the Three practices of the Attack and Defence, and word by word every movement of the foregoing detail; but it may be performed by a well-drilled class at an Inspection by simply giving the cautionary words of each practice—viz., *Cuts and Guards,* or *Points and Guards;* or *The Combination—Engage : One, Two, Three, Four—Slope Swords.*

To DISMISS THE MEN.

"On the Right (or Left) Close." | "Right (or Left) Face."
"Carry Swords." "Return Swords." | "Dismiss."

Concluding Observations.

To perfect the men in the foregoing system of Cutlass Exercise (particularly those who are likely to become Instructors), every available opportunity should be afforded to enable them to exercise their own judgment at "*Loose Play*," which may be practised as follows:—

A party of men, prepared for Attack and Defence, receive the word "Engage," when every two opponents will engage at once, and use their own judgment, but they should conform as nearly as possible to such rules and directions as the Instructor may give from time to time; a few minutes will then suffice to enable them to discover each others mode of play, when the word "*Rest*" may be given as a signal for all to cease. Every two will next play off in succession for the *first three* cuts or thrusts, in presence of the whole Class, the Instructor remarking aloud, for general information and guidance, on the good or false points of each display. When all have thus finished, the Class will again stand prepared for Attack and Defence, and be directed to face to the right, and "*change round*" one place. Finally, the two men who have won the most points should play off for the best name.

As the instructions contain all the Cuts, Guards, and Points that are necessary in actual conflict, the men should adhere, as nearly as possible, to the following rules for independent play:—

1st.—When men once "*set to*" they should keep up an earnest-like engagement, until a hit is given or received, when they are to cease for the moment, to give or receive an acknowledgment.

2nd.—The party hit is first to be careful to recover to a defensive position, and then to acknowledge by lowering his sword.

3rd.—At the moment of engaging, each party should particularly remember to be "*on guard*," so as not to be taken by surprise, and should seize the moment for an attack, so as not to risk being hit at the same instant.

4th.—Each man should endeavour, on meeting the attack, to acquire the habit of *returning instantly*, to prevent an opponent from making false attacks, or repeating a cut or point twice with impunity on closing; but he must ever be "*on guard*" to meet the impromtu hit of such as *cannot help returning*, whether hit or not.

NOTE.—"*Loose play*" can only be carried on with safety where proper skull-caps and body paddings are available; in which case, swords with hand-guards, similar to the claymore, could be employed with greater advantage and less danger than the common sticks at present in use.

BAYONET OR PIKE EXERCISE.

A PARTY of men, already trained to the Naval Cutlass and Rifle Exercise, may readily be taught the following system of Bayonet or Pike Exercise as it is based on the same principles.

The Divison being in Line, prepared for the **Manual** *Exercise.*

ATTENTION. { At the "Shoulder."

TAKE OPEN ORDER. { Front rank (if two deep) to advance eight paces, or cross the deck and face " right about."

RIGHT, ENGAGE. { "Charge Bayonets," steppin back one pace with right foot, body erect, and knees bent.

FRONT, POINT. { Point breast high, extending the arms, elbows under, and instantly prepare to repeat the same.

HIGH.
POINT.
{ At " High," elevate the point about 45°, keeping the piece close to the side, as at the " Charge."
At " Point," point high, and instantly prepare to repeat the same.

LOW.
POINT.
{ At "Low," depress the point towards the ground, keeping the piece close, as at the "Charge."
At " Point," point low, and prepare to repeat the same.

UPWARD.

POINT.
{ At " Upward," place the piece upright in front of the centre of the body, and look upward.
At " Point," point straight upward, by throwing the piece upwards to the extent of the right arm, quitting the grasp of the left hand for the moment, and prepare to repeat the same.

FORWARD.

POINT.
{ At " Forward," level the piece, look to the front, and close right foot to left, ready to advance.
At " Point," point breast high, at the same instant advance one pace with the left foot, then back again in the time of 1—2.

BAYONET EXERCISE.

BACKWARD. At "Backward," close the left foot to the right, ready to retire.

POINT. At "Point," point by throwing the piece out breast high to the extent of the right arm, quitting the grasp of the left hand for the moment, and at the same instant retire one pace with the right foot, then advance again in the time of 1—2.

COMBINE. At "Combine," close the left foot to the right, ready to repeat the last point.

POINT. At "Point," throw out the piece as before, stepping back, then advance again and deliver the forward point in the time of 1—2.

THE GUARDS.   A caution.

FIRST. Defend the head, barrel inclined upward; look to the front between the grasp of the hands, left elbow close, muzzle downward, being similar to the Cutlass 1st guard.

SECOND. Defend the right side, barrel inclined to the right, left elbow close, point downward and to the front, being similar to the Cutlass 2nd guard.

THIRD. Defend right breast and face, barrel inclined to the right, piece close to the right hip, point upwards, being similar to the Cutlass 3rd guard.

FOURTH. Defend left breast and face, barrel inclined to the left, piece still close to the right hip, point upwards, being similar to the Cutlass 4th guard, but the right arm not passed across the body.

SHOULDER ARMS. As in the "Manual Exercise."

TAKE CLOSE ORDER. Ranks close, "front" and "dress."

NOTE.—When at drill, practise the Exercise with the piece at the "Charge," on the *left* side, first giving the word, "Left Engage."

PISTOL EXERCISE.

INSTRUCTIONS

FOR THE USE OF

COLT'S REVOLVERS.

"Handle Pistol."

Seize the butt with the right hand, and draw the Pistol from the belt, then place it *upright* in the left hand, holding it round the trigger guard with the *hammer towards* and about 6 inches from the body; the thumb resting on the cylinder, ready to turn it for loading.

Note.—The principal thing to be observed in this exercise is, that the Pistol is never under any pretence to be pointed towards any one, but always kept *upright*; and when not in use the hammer is to be carefully let down to the *safety position*, between two nipples.

"Examine Pistol."

Half cock the lock with the right hand, and see if the Cylinder revolves freely, and if the Lever is in working order; then explode a cap upon each nipple, to clear them from oil or dust.

"Load."

Take a cartridge from the pouch with the right hand, strip the paper off by seizing the tape with the teeth, holding the cartridge by the bullet end, and place it in the right hand chamber; then turn the cylinder with the left thumb, until the point of the ball is brought immediately under the rammer; seize the lever with the right hand, and force the ball down *below* the surface of the cylinder, holding the butt against the chest; and so on, until all the chambers are loaded.

Note.—If any one of the chambers be turned accidentally past the rammer, before the ball is forced below the surface of the cylinder, the point of the ball should be cut off, or else the cylinder will not revolve.

Before loading, always see the nipples free from old caps, as pieces of them are liable to slip down under the cylinder, and so prevent its revolving.

"Cap."

Hold the Pistol nearly *upright* in the left hand, and press a cap on each nipple with the point of the thumb, turning the cylinder as in loading; then ease the hammer down to the *safety position*, between two nipples.

"Ready."

Seize the butt with the right hand, and cock the lock, keeping the forefinger outside the trigger guard, and the Pistol *upright*.

NOTE.—If it be desired at any time to "half cock" the lock from the "Ready," the hammer must be eased down *carefully* close to the nipple, and then pulled up to the "half cock," or else the cylinder will not revolve.

"Present."

Level the Pistol at the object with the arm slightly bent, and pull the trigger by a *steady pressure;* keeping the notch in the hammer, the foresight, and the object in one; then bring the Pistol to the left hand, keeping it *upright*, and cock the lock with the right; and so on in succession, until all the chambers are discharged.

NOTE.—If firing by order, bring the Pistol to the Capping position, and "half cock" the lock.

In the event of a "miss fire," continue the firing till all the other chambers are discharged, then "half cock" the Pistol, "re-cap," and fire as before.

"Cease Firing."

Ease the hammer down to the *safety position*.

"Return Pistol."

Seize the butt with the right hand, and return the Pistol to the belt.

NOTE.—Should anything clog or prevent the cylinder from revolving, the barrel may be taken off by forcing out the key and pressing down upon the lever, the rammer bearing upon the part between two chambers, which will force off the barrel, and allow the cylinder to be examined.

I

With DEANE *and* ADAM'S *Revolvers, the following alterations will be necessary* :—

"HANDLE PISTOL."

The same as before, except that the Pistol should be held in a manner exactly the reverse, viz., with the *trigger guard* in the hollow of the left hand, and *towards* the body; the fingers pressing the flat part of the barrel, close down to the rear sight, using the forefinger and thumb to turn the cylinder.

"THE SAFETY POSITION."

The hammer should be at "half cock;" and the small catch on the right of the lock should be pushed forward into one of the holes between the nipples made for the purpose.

"METHOD OF FIRING."

The Pistol may either be fired in the same manner as Colt's, or the chambers may be discharged in rapid succession, by simply pulling the trigger and slacking it each time.

FIELD-PIECE EXERCISE.

FIELD-PIECE EXERCISE.

The detachment fall in two deep in close order; 1 tells them off from the right, 2 being the right hand man of the rear rank, 3 the right hand man of the front rank, 4 the second man from the right of the rear rank, 5 the man in his front, and so on.

2, 4, 6, 8, 10, 12, 14, Rear Rank.
1, 3, 5, 7, 9, 11, 13, 15, Front Rank.

Posts and Duties.

(With 15 Men).

No. 1.—At the handspike; Points and Commands.
" 2.—In line with front of right wheel; Sponges.
" 3.   "   "   left wheel; Loads.
" 4.—In line with the breech; Serves the vent.
" 5.   "   "   ; Primes and fires.
" 6.—5 yards in rear of left wheel; Serves ammunition to 3.
" 7.—In rear of the limber; Serves ammunition to 8, and when firing Shell, prepares and fixes fuzes, assisted by 8.
" 8.—10 yards in rear of 6; Serves ammunition to 6, and when firing Shell, assists 7 in preparing and fixing fuzes.
" 9.—In the shafts.
" 10, 12, and 14.—With the left drag rope.
" 11, 13, and 15.—With the right drag rope.

Note.—If using match tubes, 4 carries the tube-box and primes, 5 attends the portfire, lighting it at the word "Load."

The Gun being Unlimbered.

ACTION.
> No. 1 repeats the word of command, unbuckles the handspike and ships it; 4 unbuckles the sponge, and throws it over to 2, who holds it by the centre, in his right hand.

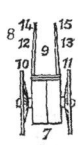

LOAD.
> No. 1 repeats the word of command, seizes the handspike with both hands, and points in the direction of the object.
>
> 2 steps in, right foot first, holding the sponge staff perpendicular by the centre with both hands; he then extends his hands, so as to bring the right hand to the rammer and the left to the sponge, forces it home with right hand, giving it two round turns; he then withdraws and capsizes the sponge, and rams home in one motion, body well thrown back.
>
> 3 steps in, left foot first, and faces the axletree; receives the ammunition from 6, and enters it when sponge is withdrawn, stepping out when gun is loaded, with 2.
>
> 4 steps in and serves the vent, forming an arch with his left elbow, to enable No. 1 to get sight of the object, and steps out again when gun is loaded.
>
> 5 holds the trigger-line, or with Friction-tubes he hooks the lanyard on to the tube ready to prime.
>
> 6 doubles to 8 for ammunition, holds it under his arm for protection in running up to the gun; and when the sponge is withdrawn, gives it to 3, then doubles to the rear for more, and resumes his position.

NOTE.—When the gun is loaded, No. 1 steps up to the breech, naming the distance and corresponding elevation, lays the gun by sight, steps smartly back, and gives the word "Ready," taking a side pace to the left, clear of the recoil; 4 then steps in, and pricks the cartridge; 5 steps in, primes, and cocks the lock, stepping out clear of recoil, with 4.

FIRE.	No. 1 repeats the word of command. 5 fires, with a steady pull if using Friction tubes; if match tubes, he holds the portfire before the vent.

NOTE.—As soon as the gun is fired, 4 steps in, clears and serves the vent. No. 1 should not give the word "Load" till this is done.

No. 2 in ramming home should brace his right shoulder and hip well in, so as to be as clear as possible in the event of explosion.

BURNT PRIMING.	No. 1 repeats the word of command. 3 steps in and faces the axletree, receives the priming wire from 4, and a tube from 5, pricks the cartridge, and primes. The gun being primed, the whole fall into their places.

CEASE FIRING.	No. 1 repeats the word of command, unships the handspike, and buckles it on to the trail. 2 passes the sponge over the axletree to 4, who buckles it on to the trail. 5 cuts an inch off the portfire, if using one. 6 returns the ammunition.

NOTE.—Whenever this order is given, the gun, if loaded, is to be fired off, ready for Limbering up.

TO RUN THE GUN AND LIMBER FORWARD OR BACK, (IN ACTION.)

PREPARE TO RUN THE GUN & LIMBER FORWARD.	No. 1 repeats the word of command; 1 and 6 seize the end of the handspike; 2, 3, 4, and 5 man the gun wheels.
MARCH.	The whole move forward.
HALT.	The whole resume their places.
PREPARE TO RUN THE GUN & LIMBER BACK.	The whole perform the same duties, facing to the rear.

LIMBERING UP.

(May be done either to the Front, Rear, Right, or Left.)

FRONT LIMBER UP.
> No. 1 repeats the word of command; 1 and 6 lift the trail, and carry it to the "left about," 2, 3, 4, and 5 assisting at the wheels; when the trail is round, the whole fall into their places within the wheels; 2 and 3 with their backs to the axletree, between the chase and the wheels; 4 and 5 with their backs to the axletree, between the breech and the wheels; 1 and 6 in their front.
>
> The limber comes up to the right of the gun, and when it is square 1 gives the word "Halt," "Limber up;" 1 and 6 lift the trail by the handles; 2, 3, 4, and 5 man the gun wheels, 7 and 8 the limber wheels; when the trail is on the pintail, 1 keys it, and gives the word "Form the Order of March."

REAR LIMBER UP.
> The same Nos. perform the same duties, but the limber reverses to its left as soon as it arrives at the trail, which is not thrown round.

RIGHT (or Left) LIMBER UP.
> The same as before; but the trail and limber go to the right or left.

Unlimbering or Coming into Action.

(May be done either to the Front, Rear, Right, or Left; and is the reverse of "Limbering up.")

Action Front.
: No. 1 repeats the word of command, and unkeys the pintail; 1 and 6 lift the trail, as in limbering up; 2, 3, 4, and 5 man the gun wheels; 7 and 8 the limber wheels. When the trail is clear, 1 gives the word "Drive on;" the limber goes off to the "left about," the trail to the "right about."

When the trail is round, 1 unbuckles the handspike and ships it; 4 unbuckles the sponge, and throws it over to 2; when the limber is sufficiently to the rear, it reverses to its left, and halts 15 yards in rear of, and covering the gun.

Action Right (Left, or Rear).
: The gun is unlimbered by the same Nos. and upon the same principle as in coming into Action to the Front.

Retreating with the Prolonge.

Load. Prepare to Retreat with the Prolonge.
: No. 1 repeats the word of command; the limber comes up, and reverses to its left, 3 yards from the trail; 6 and 7 take the prolonge down; 6 hooks it on to the trail plate eye; and 7 to the pintail.

The Battery will Retire.
: The limber moves off at once. No. 1 gives the order "Right about face;" the whole face to the rear, keeping one yard from the wheels; 2 carries the sponge in left hand; 3 steps in, receives the priming wire from 4, and forces it down the vent to keep the cartridge home.

Halt. Fire.
: No. 1 gives the order "Front," and proceeds to lay the gun; 2 steps in, and rams home; 4 serves the vent.

FIELD-PIECE EXERCISE.

THE BATTERY WILL RETIRE LOAD. { No. 2 follows the gun whilst loading; 3 serves the vent, and forces the priming wire down to keep the cartridge home; 6 enters ammunition.

HALT. UNHOOK PROLONGE. { Nos. 6 and 7 unhook and make up prolonge; 7 orders "Drive on," and the limber goes to the rear.

NOTE.—If desired, the following order may be given, "Cease Firing," "Unhook Prolonge," "Limber up."

ADVANCING WITH THE PROLONGE.

PREPARE TO ADVANCE WITH THE PROLONGE. { No. 1 repeats the word of command; 2, 3, and 4 step in under cover; the limber comes up to the right of the gun; 6 assists 1 at the handspike; 7 takes down the prolonge, and places the centre ring over the pintail; 2 and 3 hook on to the breast chains or loop.

HALT. ACTION. { No. 1 repeats the word of command; 3 steps in, unhooks the prolonge, and orders "Drive on;" 6 and 7 make it up; the limber reverses to its left, and goes to the rear; 5 stepping in under cover.

TO DISMOUNT A LIGHT 12-POUNDER HOWITZER.

No. 1 unships the handspike, and places it five yards to the right.

2 carries the sponge five yards to the right; and 5 the portfire five yards to the left.

2 and 3 take off the cap squares.

4 and 5 steady and man the wheels.

1, 6, and 7 raise the trail.

2 and 3, when the muzzle reaches the ground, pull the gun out of the trunnion boxes, and steady it on its muzzle.

1, 6, and 7 lower the trail, but not to the ground, until the carriage has been run five yards to the rear.

2 and 3 lower the gun to the ground, vent uppermost.

To Dismount the Carriage.

Nos. 4 and 5 take out linch-pins, and take off washers; 2 and 3 in front, inside of the wheels, lift the carriage. 4 and 5 in rear, inside of the wheels, lift the carriage. 6 and 8 take off the right wheel; 6 in front, 8 in rear. 7 and 9 take off the left wheel; 7 in front, 9 in rear.

To Dismount the Limber.

Nos. 10 and 11 lift at the splinter-bar; 12 and 13 at the rear part of the limber; 14 and 15 take out the linch-pins, take off the washers and wheels. The whole is then lowered on the ground, the Nos. sitting on their work.

NOTE.—Should it be necessary to have 17 men, 16 and 17 will assist 14 and 15 in taking off the wheels.

To Mount the Limber.

Everything will be replaced by the same Nos.

To Mount the Carriage.

Everything will be replaced by the same Nos.

To Mount the Gun.

All the Nos. assist to raise the gun on its muzzle; 2 and 3 steady it there. The carriage is then run up to the gun by 1, 6, and 7, at the trail; 4 and 5 at the wheels. At the word "Up trail," 1, 6, and 7 raise the trail; 2 and 3 force the gun into the trunnion boxes; 1, 6, and 7 pull down the trail; 1 ships the handspike; 2 and 3 put on the cap squares; 2 immediately gets the sponge ready for loading, and 5 the portfire.

NOTE.—The 24-pounder Howitzer, with 20 men, is dismounted in a similar manner.

CHANGING ROUNDS.

With a Full Crew.				With Gun Nos. only.			
No.	1	becomes	5	No.	1	becomes	5
,,	5	,,	3	,,	5	,,	3
,,	3	,,	2	,,	3	,,	2
,,	2	,,	4	,,	2	,,	4
,,	4	,,	15	,,	4	,,	9
,,	15	,,	13	,,	9	,,	7
,,	13	,,	11	,,	7	,,	8
,,	11	,,	10	,,	8	,,	6
,,	10	,,	12	And ,,	6	,,	1
,,	12	,,	14				
,,	14	,,	9				
,,	9	,,	7				
,,	7	,,	8				
,,	8	,,	6				
And ,,	6	,,	1				

NOTE.—In the event of any number at the gun being disabled, the highest No. of the detachment is to take his place, except in the case of No. 1, when the best man should be selected.

Ranges with Brass Ordnance.

Elevation by Tangent-Sight.

Nature of Gun.	Diameter of Bore.	Windage	Weight of Shot or Spherical Case.	Charge.	Elevation and Range in Yards, with corresponding Lengths of Fuze.												
	In.	In.	Sph. Case	lbs.	$\frac{1}{4}°$	$\frac{1}{2}°$	$\frac{3}{4}°$	1°	$1\frac{1}{2}°$	2°	$2\frac{1}{2}°$	3°	$3\frac{1}{2}°$	4°	$4\frac{1}{2}°$	5°	6°
Howitzer. 24-Pr. 4 ft. 8 in. 12½ cwt.	5·72	·12	20 lbs.	2½	250	300	350	400	500	600	700	800	900	1000	1100	1200	1350
			No. of Balls 100	Burster. 3 ozs.		·1	·1	·15	·2	·25	·35	·45	·55	·65	·75	·85	1·0

These Ranges may also be used for the Hollow Shot and Shell.

					$\frac{5}{8}°$	$\frac{7}{8}°$	$1\frac{1}{8}°$	$1\frac{3}{8}°$	2°	$2\frac{1}{2}°$	3°	$3\frac{1}{2}°$	4°	$4\frac{1}{2}°$	5°	6°	7°
Howitzer. 12 Pr. 4 ft. 6 in. 10 cwt.	4·58	·12	Shot. 12 lbs.	2 lbs.	200	300	400	500	650	800	950	1050	1150	1250	1350	1550	1700
				Burster. 1 oz. 12 drs.	·1	·15	·2	·25	·35	·5	·6	·7	·8	·9	1·0		

These Ranges may also be used for the Spherical Case and Common Shell.

RANGES.

Howitzer.	Charge		Projectile		Elevations												
12-Pr. 3 ft. 9 in. 6½ cwt.	4·58	·12	Sph. Case 10 lbs. No. of Balls 75	1¼ lbs. Burster 1 oz. 12 drs.	½°	¾°	1°	1½°	2°	2½°	3°	3⅜°	3¾°	4⅛°	4½°	5°	6°
				Range	250	300	350	450	550	650	700	750	800	850	900	950	1050
				Time	·1	·1	·15	·2	·3	·4	·45	·5	·6	·6	·65	·7	·8

These Ranges may also be used for the Hollow Shot and Shell.

Gun.	Charge		Projectile		Elevations											
6-Pr. 5 ft. 6 cwt.	3·66	·12	Sph. Case 5 lbs. No. of Balls 30	1¼ lbs. Burster 12 drs.	¼°	½°	¾°	1°	1½°	2°	2½°	3°	3¾°	4½°	5¼°	6°
				Range	300	400	500	600	700	800	900	1000	1100	1200	1300	1400
				Time	·1	·15	·2	·25	·3	·4	·5	·6	·7	·8	·9	1·0

These Ranges may also be used for the Shot.

NOTE.—In firing Spherical Case from heavy guns, the Charges, Elevations, and Times of Flight may be taken as for Common Shell.

FIELD BATTERY DRILL.

Preliminary Observations.

1. A Battery has no fixed right or left, and only acknowledges the front to which the guns point when in Action, or the detachment's face when "limbered up;" but when a Battery is *inverted*, the Commanding Officer should make use of the words "Present Right" (or Left) as necessary.

2. A Battery in Column should not present a smaller front than that of Divisions, except for passing obstacles or route marching.

3. A Battery "limbered up" should always dress *forward*, and if too far advanced, it must reverse and come up to the alignment. In Action the dressing is on the axletree of the gun on which the formation is made.

4. As a general rule the guns of a Battery in Action should not be discharged at once, but a continuous fire be kept up, and they should be directed on some named object in front.

5. When a *Battery in Line* is ordered for Action, the guns are not to be loaded until the word "Load" is given by the Commanding Officer, and when loaded they are to wait for the order to fire.

6. When the guns are formed in *"Line for Action"* in *succession*, they are loaded and fired as soon as formed, unless ordered to the contrary; and they continue Independent firing until ordered to "Cease firing."

7. When a Battery is ordered to fire a certain number of rounds, the firing should commence from the right or left of Batteries or Half batteries, by which a regular and continued fire will be maintained.

8. When guns are in Action and the word "Cease firing" is given, all guns then loaded are to be fired off (provided your own force is not in front), and on no account is a gun to be "limbered up" or to move whilst loaded.

9. A Battery, when acting with troops, should conform to their movements, and proceed to its position in the simplest and most expeditious manner. It however should remain in rear of any intended alignment until the troops are finally formed.

10. The Artillery should always cover the troops when Advancing, Retiring or Deploying into line.

11. When the Line retires by alternate Companies, Wings, or Battalions, the Artillery must remain with that part of it which is nearest the enemy, retiring with the prolonge, and halting when it arrives at the halted part of the line.

12. When the troops are in Column, the Artillery should be on the *reverse* flank; when in Line, they are usually posted on the flanks or centre.

13. When a line of troops wheel *backwards* into Column, the Artillery break into Column and close to the *reverse* flank, so as not to interrupt the line of pivots.

14. In retreating the Artillery may retire in Line, or by Half batteries, or by Divisions, forming new lines, and retreating again, or it may retreat *alternately*. This must depend on the nature of the ground, and the flank on which the enemy may be.

Telling off and Proving the Battery.

The crews fall in with their guns "Limbered up," and in Line, at full intervals of 15 yards, No. 1 gun being on the right. The Battery is then proved as follows:—

"Call numbers."   "Tell off by subdivisions from the right."
(*The Nos.* 1 *here call Sub.* 1, *Sub.* 2, *Sub.* 3, *and so on.*)
" Subd. 1 and 2 are the 1st or Right Division."
"   „   3 and 4   „   the 2nd or Centre Division."
"   „   5 and 6   „   the 3rd or Left Division."
"   „   1, 3, and 5 are the Right Guns of Divisions."
"   „   2, 4, and 6   „   the Left Guns of Divisions."
"   „   3 and 4 are the two Centre Subdivisions."
"   „   1, 2, and 3 are the Right Half Battery."
"   „   4, 5, and 6   „   the Left Half Battery."
"   „   1 and 4 are the Right Guns of Half Batteries."
"   „   2 and 5   „   the Centre Guns."
"   „   3 and 6   „   the Left Guns."

Note.—The Battery is then proved by naming a Subdivision, Division, or Half Battery, or any one individual number of the Gun Detachment; at the word "Prove" every man of the named Subdivision, Division, or Half Battery, raises the right arm, keeping it up until the word "Down" is given.

Posts of Officers.

Commanding Officer.	When in Line "Limbered up"	In front of the Centre.
,,	When in Column	On the Pivot Flank, or where most needed.
,,	When in Action	In rear of the Centre.
Officers.	When in Line "Limbered up"	The *Senior* on the right of the Right Division; the *Second* on the left of the Left Division; the *Junior* on the right of the Centre Division.
,,	When in Column of Route	On the Pivot Flanks of their leading Subdivisions.
,,	When in Column of Divisions	On the Pivot Flanks of their respective Divisions.
,,	When in Column of Half Batteries	The Officer of Centre Division on the Pivot Flank of the leading Half Battery; the others, as when in Line "limbered up."
,,	When in Action	Between the guns of their Divisions, a little in rear.

NOTE.—In shifting from one flank to the other, the Officers always pass along the front at the "double."

By the term "Pivot Flank" is to be understood that flank upon which a Division or Half Battery must be wheeled, when in column, to reform line; the other is called the "Reverse Flank:" therefore, when *right* is in front, *left* is the pivot, and *vice versa.*

MANŒUVRES OF A FIELD BATTERY OF SIX GUNS.

NOTE.—The following Manœuvres will also answer for a Battery of Four Guns, except "Deploying into Line," when the 2nd Division must act as the 3rd Division with Six Guns. The most simple and useful Manœuvres for Actual Service are those marked *.

COMMANDING OFFICER. Repeated by Officers.	OFFICERS OF DIVISIONS AND SUBDIVISIONS.

* BATTERY IN LINE TO ADVANCE.

THE BATTERY WILL ADVANCE. MARCH. { The Subdivision of direction and the pace should be named by the Commanding Officer.

* TO RETIRE.

RIGHT (or Left) REVERSE. MARCH. { Reversing when in Column should be done *from* the Pivot flank.

NOTE.—In reversing with Quarter intervals, the Right Guns of Divisions move forward their own length, the others halting; the whole then reverse together, and the Line is reformed.

TO DIMINISH (OR INCREASE) INTERVALS ON THE MARCH.

HALF (Q^r. or Full) INTERVALS ON SUBDIVISION — { Each Subdivision (except the one named) "Right or Left half turn," "Front turn."

NOTE.—Much used in Brigade Movements, and recommended generally in the Field, especially when acting without waggons.

* TO TAKE GROUND TO A FLANK.

RIGHT (or Left) TAKE GROUND. MARCH. { This can only be done at "Full intervals."

NOTE.—Line can be quickly formed to the Front from this position by the order "To the Right or Left of the Front form Line," or the Guns can be brought into Action on either Flank, by the order, "Action Right or Left."

TO MAKE A "HALF TURN" ON THE MARCH.

RIGHT (or Left) HALF TURN. FRONT TURN. { Subdivision 1 makes the "half turn" correctly; the leader of Subdivision 2 dresses by the axletree of Subdivison 1, and about 11 yards distant; the leader of 3 dresses by the axletree of 2 and so on.

K

| Commanding-Officer. Repeated by Officers. | Officers of Divisions and Subdivisions. |

* (1.) From Column of Route, *Right in Front*, to form Column of Divisions on the March.

Form Column of Divisions. { Subdivisions 2, 4, 6, "Left half turn," "Double," "Front turn."

* (2.) To form Column of Route on the March.

Form Column of Route. { Subdivisions 2, 4, 6, "Right half turn," "Front turn," the whole following each other in succession.

* (3.) From Column of Route, *Left in Front*, to form Column of Divisions on the March.

Form Column of Divisions. { Subdivisions 5, 3, 1, "Right half turn," "Double," "Front turn."

* (4.) To form Column of Route on the March.

Form Column of Route. { Subdivisions 5, 3, 1, "Left half turn," "Front turn," the whole following each other in succession.

* (5.) From Column of Divisions, *Left in Front*, to form Line to the Left.

Form Line to the Left on the Leading Division. March. { Left Division, "Left Wheel," "Halt." Centre and Right Division "Right half turn," "Front turn," "Left Wheel," "Halt," "Dress," in line with Left Division.

Note.—Forming Line to the Right when *Right in front* is done on the same principle.

(6.) To form Column of Divisions in Rear of the Right.

Form Column of Divisions in Rear of the Right. March. { Centre Division, "Right reverse," "Left take ground" twice, "Halt" in rear of Right Division. Left Division, "Right reverse," "Left half turn" twice, "Left take ground," "Halt" in rear of Centre Division.

Note.—Forming Column of Divisions in rear of the *Left* is done on the same principle.

No. 1.

From Column of Route, Right in front to form Column of Divisions.

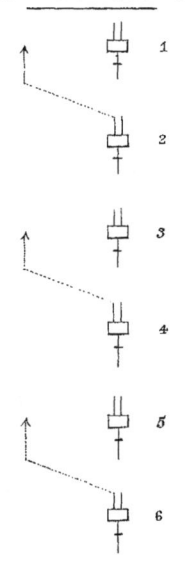

No. 3.

From Column of Route, Left in front to form Column of Divisions.

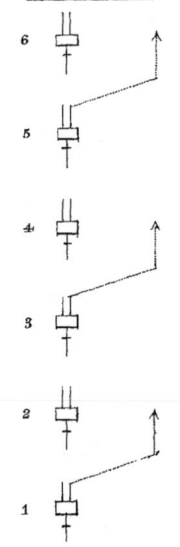

No. 5.

From Column of Divisions Left in front to form line to the Left.

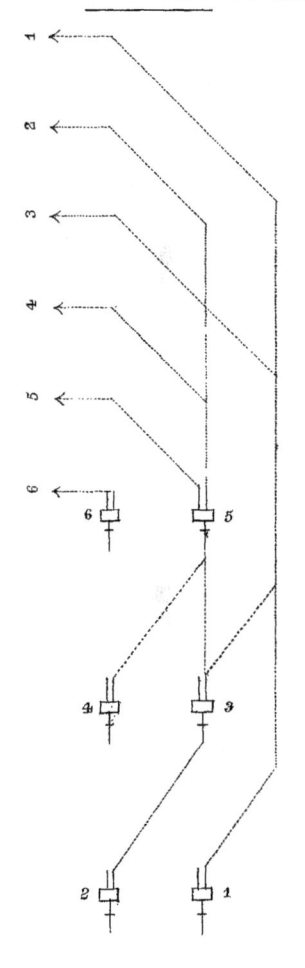

N⁰ 7.

From Column of Divisions Right in front to form line to the Left.

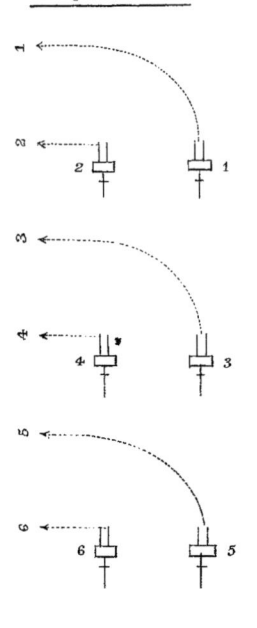

N⁰ 8.

To advance from the Right in a Column of Divisions

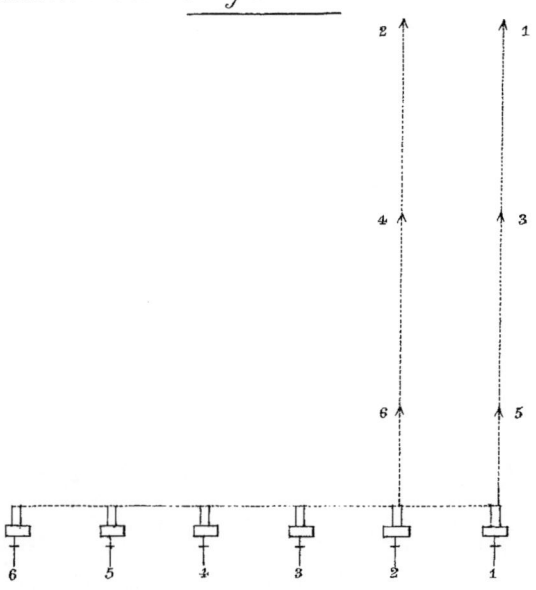

Nº 6.

To form Column of Divisions in rear of the Right.

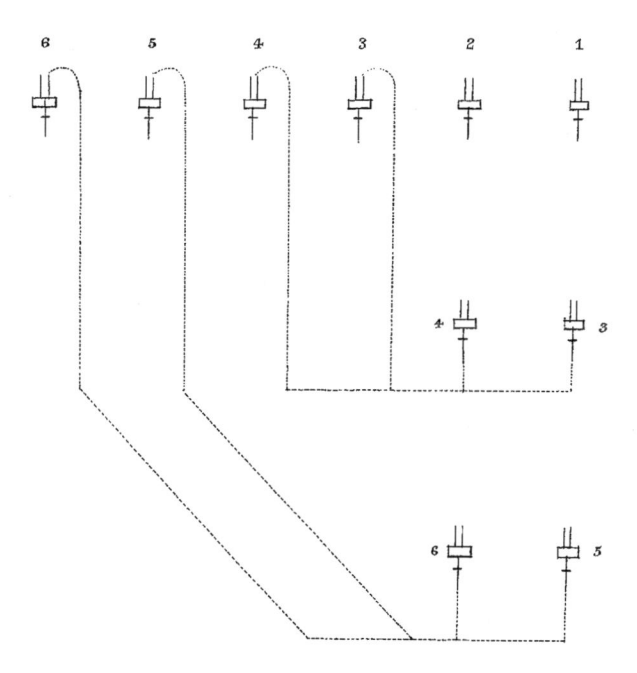

Nº 9.

From Column of Divisions Right in Front to form line to the Front.

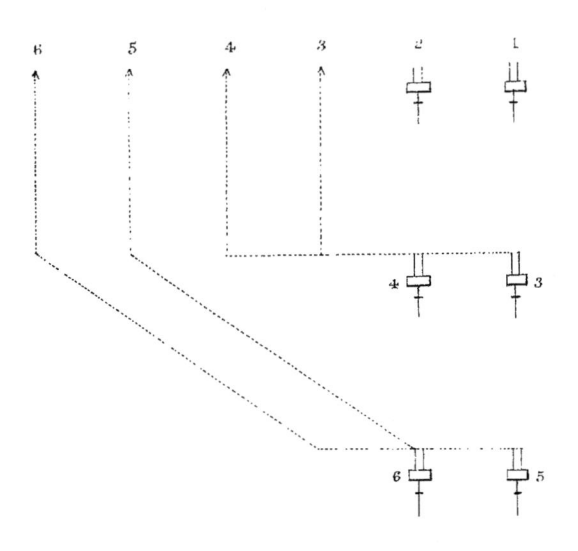

Nº 10.

To advance from the Centre in a double Column of Subdivisions.

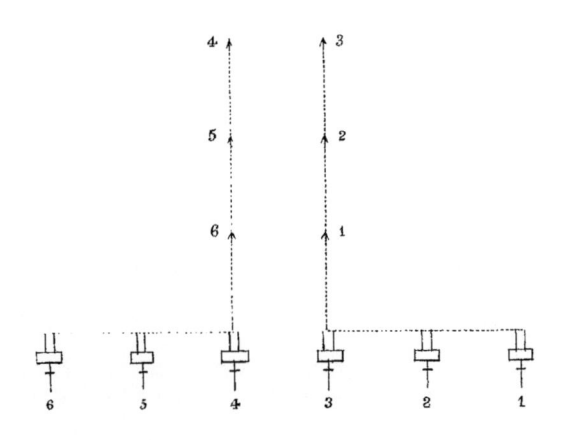

FIELD BATTERY DRILL. 131

| Commanding Officer. Repeated by Officers. | Officers of Divisions and Subdivisions. |

*(7.) From Column of Divisions, *Right in Front*, to form Line to the Left on the March.

Line to the Left. Divisions Left Wheel. { Each Division wheels to the left on its Pivot Subdivision, "Halt," when in Line.

Note.—If ordered to form "*Line for Action*," the Pivot Subdivisions come at once into "Action Left;" the remainder "Left Wheel;" and then "Action Front." Forming Line to the Right when *Left in front* is done on the same principle.

"Action Front," "Load," "Commence Firing from the Right of Half Batteries," "Cease Firing," "Front Limber up."

(8.) To advance from a Flank in a Column of Divisions.

Advance from the Right in a Column of Divisions. March. { Right Division "Forward." Centre and Left Divisions "Right take ground." And when in rear of Right Division, "Left take ground."

Note.—Advancing from the *Left* is done on the same principle.

(9.) From Column of Divisions, *Right in Front*, to form Line to the Front for Action.

To the Left of the Front form Line for Action. March. "Cease Firing." "Front Limber up." { Right Division "Action Front." Centre Division "Left take ground," "Right take ground," "Halt," "Action Front." Left Division "Left take ground," "Right half turn" twice, "Halt," "Action Front."

Note.—Forming Line when *Left in front* is done on the same principle.

(10.) To advance from the Centre in a Double Column of Subdivisions.

Advance from the Centre in a Double Column of Subdivisions. March. { Two Centre Subdivisions "Forward." Subdivisions 2 and 1 "Left take ground" and "Right take ground." Subdivisions 5 and 6 "Right take ground,' "Left take ground," following in rear of the two Centre Subdivisions.

K 2

| Commanding Officer. Repeated by Officers. | Officers of Divisions and Subdivisions. |

(11.) From Double Column of Subdivisions to form Line to the Front for Action.

Right and Left of the Front form Line for Action. March. "Cease Firing." "FrontLimberup."
{ Two Centre Subdivisions "Action Front." Subdivisions 2 and 1 "Right half turn," "Front turn," "Halt," "Action Front." Subdivisions 5 and 6 "Left half turn," "Front turn," "Halt," "Action Front." }

(12.) From Double Column of Subdivisions to form Line to a Flank.

Form Line to the Right on the Right Half Battery. March.
{ Subdivisions 3, 2, and 1, "Right wheel," "Halt." Subdivisions 4, 5, and 6, "Forward," "Right wheel," "Halt," "Dress." }

Note.—Forming line to the *Left* on the Left half Battery is done on the same principle.

"Action Front," "Dismount the Battery," "Mount the Battery," "Commence Firing from the two Centre Subdivisions," "Cease Firing," "Front Limber up."

(13.) Battery in Line to break into Column to a Flank.

Break into Column of Divisions to the Right. March.
{ Subdivisions 1, 3, 5, "Right wheel," and "Halt." Subdivisions 2, 4, 6, "Forward," "Right wheel," "Halt," and "Dress" on Subdivisions 1, 3, 5. }

Note.—This movement would generally be employed to march past with other Troops, and with Half Batteries at reduced intervals.
Breaking into Column to the *Left* is done on the same principle.

(14.) Divisions, *Right in Front*, to deploy on the Rear Division.

Deploy on the Rear Division. March.
{ Right Division "Right take ground" twice, "Right reverse," "Halt." Centre Division "Right take ground," "Left take ground," "Halt." Left Division "Forward," "Double," "Halt," "Dress." }

Note.—Deploying with Divisions *Left in front* is done on the same principle.
All deployments are on the front base.

Nº 11.

From double Column of Subdivisions to form line to the Front.

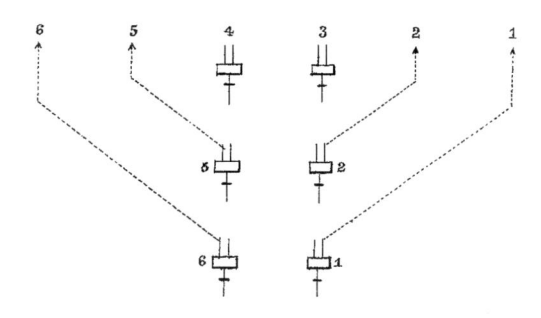

Nº 12.

From double Column of Subdivisions to form line to the Right.

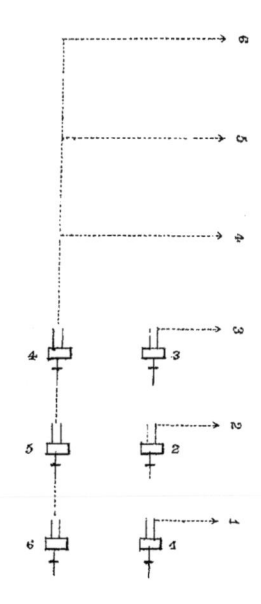

Nº 13.

To break into Column of Divisions to the Right.

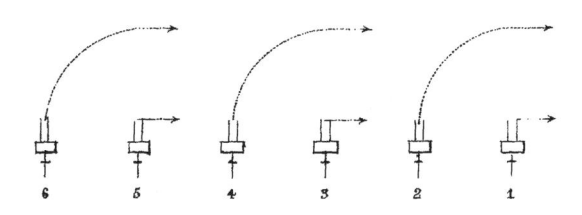

Nº 14.

Divisions Right in front to deploy on the Rear Division

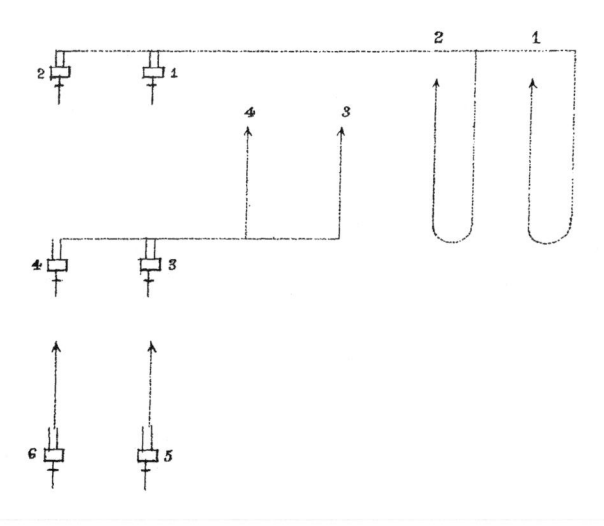

Nº 15.

Divisions Right in front to deploy on the Centre Division

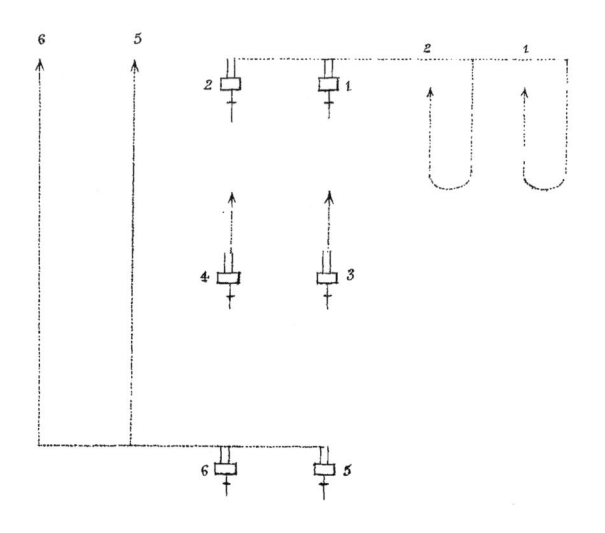

Nº 18.

To change front to the Right

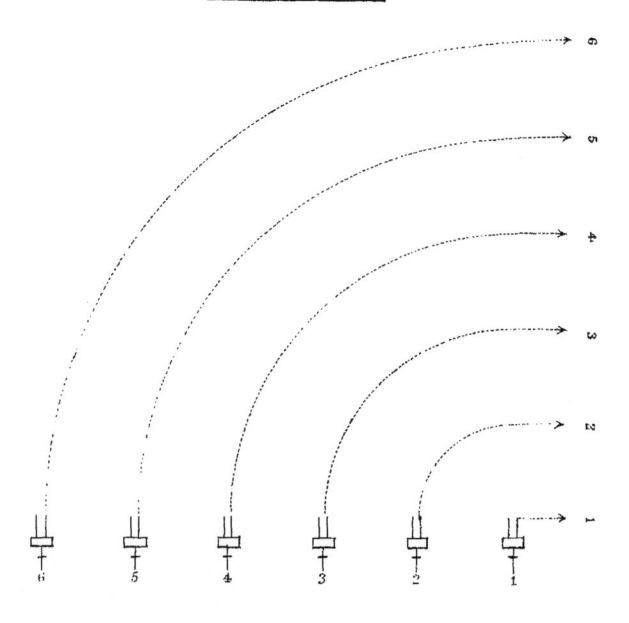

COMMANDING OFFICER. *Repeated by Officers.*	OFFICERS OF DIVISIONS AND SUBDIVISIONS.

(15.) DIVISIONS, *Right in Front,* TO DEPLOY ON THE CENTRE DIVISION.

DEPLOY ON THE CENTRE DIVISION. MARCH.
{ Right Division "Right take ground" twice, "Right reverse," "Halt." Centre Division "Forward," "Double," "Halt." Left Division "Left take ground," "Right take ground," "Halt," "Dress." }

NOTE.—Deploying on the Centre Division when *Left in Front* is done on the same principle.

(16.) TO DEPLOY INTO LINE FOR ACTION.

DEPLOY ON THE REAR (or Centre) DIVISION FOR ACTION. MARCH. "Cease Firing."
{ The Divisions all proceed as before, except that the Leading Division, instead of going to the rear and reversing, comes into action to the Right or Left when in its place; the other Divisions coming into action to the Front. }

*(17.) BATTERY IN LINE TO RETIRE BY ALTERNATE SUBDIVISIONS IN ACTION.

RETIRE BY ALTERNATE SUBDIVISIONS FROM THE RIGHT. "Cease Firing."
{ Subd. 1, 3, 5, "Rear Limber up," "March," and when 20 yards in rear "Halt," "Action Rear."
Subd. 2, 4, 6, (when 1, 3, 5, have come into action), "Rear Limber up," "March," and when 20 yards in rear of 1, 3, 5, "Halt," "Action Rear;" and so on in succession, until ordered to "Cease Firing." }

NOTE.—The *retired* Guns reserve their fire till those in advance have limbered up and retired through them.
The Limbers should not reverse, but pull off a few yards clear of the Trail ready to Limber up quickly.
At "Cease Firing," the whole will "Rear limber up" and reform line.
The above would be generally practised with the Prolonge. Retiring by Half Batteries or Divisions is done on the same principle.

*(18.) BATTERY IN LINE TO CHANGE FRONT TO A FLANK.

CHANGE FRONT TO THE RIGHT ON No. 1. MARCH.
{ Subdivision 1 "Right wheel," "Halt."
Subdivisions 2, 3, 4, 5, 6, "Left Shoulders," "Halt," "Dress." }

NOTE.—If ordered to "*Change front for Action,*" the Pivot Gun comes at once into Action in the new direction, the remainder as before, and then "Action Front."
Changing front to the *Left* is done on the same principle.

SCALING LADDER EXERCISE.

ALL Ships should carry four ladders, numbered 1, 2, 3, 4.
All Sloops should carry two ladders, numbered 1, 2.
Length—half the length of the waist netting, not less than 20 feet.
Width—as wide as the waist netting will admit.
To be fitted with toggles and loops on both ends, for fastening all together.
Four men to be stationed to each ladder, numbered 1, 2, 3, 4, 1 and 2 to the heel; 3 and 4 to the head of the ladder.
A Petty officer in charge of the first two ladders, and another of the two last. The first leads when the ladders are prepared for action. Ladders are to be carried with their heels foremost, and steps downwards.

At the order "*Prepare for Action.*"

No. 1 ladder is laid on the ground to the right, No. 2 next to it, then No. 3, and No. 4 on the left. All are then toggled together.
When ordered to "Shoulder," the same men carry the ladders.

At the order "*Plant Ladders.*"

The ladders are to be planted with the heels about 5 feet from the wall, the leading men going inside of them, and placing their feet against the heels, assist the raising with their hands. The rear men raise the ladders till perpendicular, then press with their feet to prevent slipping, until the ladders are lowered.
The ladder men attend the ladders until the storming party scale, and then follow, unless ordered to the contrary.
If ladders of great length are required, No. 2 is placed under No. 1, No. 4 under No. 3, half locked with each other; the two ladders are then toggled and seized together with spun-yarn. The four ladders thus made into two are then worked as before.

FIELD FORTIFICATION.

FIELD FORTIFICATION.

A FEW practical remarks for facilitating the throwing up of a Battery or other Fieldwork by a party of Seamen, with such materials as are likely to be at their disposal.

To make the same construction apply to a Redoubt as well as a Battery, the latter must be considered to be an elevated Battery (that in most general use), being traced upon the natural level, and presenting a complete parapet.

When under fire, and immediate cover consequently necessary, a *trench* is dug, and the earth hastily thrown up in the form of a parapet *towards* the enemy, as in sieges; hence the word "trenches," the lines of parapet thus raised, are termed "parallels," from their position with regard to the point of attack. A trench differs from a ditch, inasmuch as it is an excavation in *rear* of a parapet, instead of in advance of it.

In excavating the trenches the workmen are covered and protected by gabions filled with earth; this process is called "sapping."

To construct works according to the rules laid down in this paper, the workmen must avail themselves of the cover of night, or not be in actual presence or range of an enemy.

MATERIALS.

The working party should be provided with the following materials, viz.:—

1st. A measuring tape or chain; a protractor; a T-square; and about 24 pickets for *tracing* the Redoubt or Battery.

2nd. About 24 hedge stakes or battens, length varying from 8 to 12 feet, saws, hatchets, and a ball of rope or spunyarn for *profiling.*

3rd. Sandbags, casks or planks, with upright timbers for *revetting*. (If the latter be used, hammers and nails will be necessary.)

To find the number of sandbags required, let H be the height (in feet) to be revetted and L the length; then, since 16 bags revet 10 superficial feet, therefore

$$\frac{8\ H\ L}{5} = \text{number of bags.}$$

to which add *one-fourth* to compensate for their perishable nature.

The number of casks required must of course depend upon their size and diameter (being arranged in tiers like gabions). A party landing from a ship might be accompanied by the cooper with a boatload of *shakes*, when a good and speedy revetment might be obtained. The casks would also be especially useful for the construction of Traverses.

4th. The working party must be plentifully supplied with *pickaxes, shovels,* and *rammers*. Upon arriving at the spot selected for constructing the work, they should be told off in squads, and have their several duties assigned them by the Officer in charge.

Tracing.

The position of the Battery or Redoubt being determined upon, as well as its *extent*, which, for the first, will depend upon the number of guns intended to be placed in position; and for the latter, upon the number of men available for defence; remembering that guns are usually 18 feet apart in *Battery,* and that each file requires *one lineal yard* of parapet where musketry fire is intended. Assuming the *command* to be $7\frac{1}{2}$ feet, the least height of parapets on level ground (proceed as follows):—

1st. Measure with the tape or chain the *crest* line on each face, marking the angles with pickets, and laying them off with the protractor, connecting the pickets by lines scored with a pickaxe.

2ndly. Set off externally from the *crest* line (on each face), at right angles to it with the T-square, the *thickness* of parapet; which is regulated by the calibre of the artillery it is intended to resist, the degree of permanency required, and the time available for excavation, and varies from 6 to 24 feet; 18 feet being required to resist 24 pounders.

3rdly. Measure in like manner the *base* of the *exterior* slope, equal to its height, *less* than the *command* of the work by *one-sixth* of the thickness of parapet, or *one-twelfth*, if no musketry fire is required.

4thly. Measure the *berm*, 2 feet in ordinary soil.

5thly. Show the *escarp* and *counterscarp* lines, which will determine the *width* of the ditch at the *top;* the escarp and counterscarp usually have a slope of *one-third* and *one-fourth* the *depth* of the ditch respectively; the *escarp* has the greater slope, having (assisted by the berm) to support the weight of the parapet.

The depth and width of ditches is regulated chiefly by the quantity of earth required to build the parapet. If the ditch be not intended for an obstacle, but merely to obtain the necessary amount of earth, as is frequently the case in Batteries, a *broad* and *shallow* ditch is recommended, the labour of throwing up the earth being thus materially lessened. The limits should be 12 feet depth, and 20 feet width.

The different measurements *outwards* from the *crest* being now obtained, set off *internally* at right angles as before.

1st. The *base* of the *interior* slope, about 1 foot or ¼th its height.

2ndly. The *tread* of the *banquette* (when musketry fire is intended), 3 feet for one rank, 4 feet 6 inches for two ranks.

3rdly. The *base* of the slope of the *banquette, twice* its height, (4 feet 3 inches *less* than the *command* of the work): when this slope would take up too much interior space it is made steeper, and the banquette ascended by steps cut in it.

Having now completed the measurements on either side of the crest line upon each face; through the points thus obtained, draw lines parallel to it with a pickaxe, and produce them till they meet at the different angles; both exterior and interior space may sometimes be gained with advantage by rounding off the junction of the several lines at the various angles.

Profiling.

Two or more profiles are set up upon each face at right angles to the crest, showing the height and form of the Parapet, as follows:—

1st. Let the first stake be planted on the *crest* line, and make it equal in height to the *command* of the work (allowing for the part imbedded in the earth). *See* Fig.

2ndly. Plant the second stake on the line in the plan, showing the *thickness* of parapet, and let it be shorter than the *first* by *one-sixth* the thickness of parapet, or *one-twelfth*, as the case may require. Connect the tops of these stakes with rope-yarn, and bring the end down to a picket on the line traced in the plan for the *base* of the *exterior* slope.

3rdly. The *superior* and *exterior* slopes being thus shown, if no banquette is required, show the *interior* slope, by connecting the top of the stake first planted with a picket on the line, showing the *base* of the *interior* slope in the plan.

But if a banquette be necessary, then set up a third stake on this line, shorter than the *first* by 4 feet 3 inches; and on the line in the plan showing the tread of the banquette, erect a fourth stake 2 inches shorter than the *third* (that the *tread* may have a slight slope to the rear, for drainage); connect the tops of these last stakes, and bring the end down to a picket on the line showing the *base* of the slope of the *banquette*; the Profile of the parapet and banquette will be complete, and be thus represented:

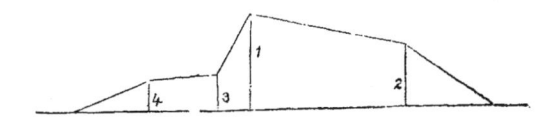

Revetting.

Newly dug earth will seldom stand unsupported at a less angle than 45°; therefore, when it is necessary that the slope should be *steeper*, it must be strengthened, or revetted.

The simplest and speediest revetment is effected with *sand-bags;* they are laid in tiers alternately, headers and stretchers; that is, at right angles, and parallel to the crest of the parapet (necks inwards); they should be only about *three-fourths* filled, and loosely tied, so that they may be easily flattened with a spade, and made to lay closely together; in filling them, care should be taken to avoid shingle, otherwise, if struck by a shot, they might wound those they were intended to cover.

Sand-bags are not generally used for revetting *embrasures*, as the explosion would frequently burst them, and they would also be liable to be ignited, especially when tarred, which is recommended to be done to render them more durable.

Batteries are sometimes built entirely of sand-bags, a most expeditious method when the supply of bags is very large. Some idea of the number required to build a Battery can be obtained from the knowledge that *fifty bags build one cubic yard*. A sand-bag, when *quite full*, contains about one *cubic foot;* they are bushel bags, 2 feet 8 inches long, by 1 foot 4 inches wide.

Casks are used as gabions, placed in the parapet at the slope of revetment, and filled with earth. Number depending upon the height of revetment, and their height and diameter, as before stated.

Planks, when used for revetment, are nailed to upright timbers, which are planted against the parapet at the required slope. This is especially an *escarp* revetment, and would be the best to apply to the *cheeks* of embrasures, when limited to he materials named in page 137.

EMBRASURES.

The parapet must first be raised to the height required for the *soles* of the embrasures, usually about 3 feet (depending upon the nature of the ordnance to be used), then proceed as follows:—

Draw a line across the solid of the parapet, at right angles to the crest, to represent the centre or *axis* of the embrasure; and on each side of the line measure under the *interior* crest *half* the width of the neck (the whole width being from 2 to 3 feet usually); then under the *exterior* crest set off *one-fourth* the thickness of the parapet on each side of the *axis* (the usual width of the mouth of the embrasure being about *one-half* the thickness of the parapet); join the measurements thus obtained at the neck and mouth, and the cheeks or sides of the embrasure will be traced.

Embrasures need not be revetted for more than 10 or 12 feet. At the neck, the revetment is kept nearly perpendicular, to protect the gunners as much as possible, and at 10 or 12 feet a *base* equal to *half* the height is sufficient for the slope.

The soles of the embrasures should have a slight slope *outwards* for depression.

TRAVERSES.

In situations likely to be exposed to enfilade fire, Traverses of earth about 16 feet in length, and from 10 to 12 feet thick, may be thrown up with advantage between the guns; but splinter-proof Traverses, 2 feet from the parapet, and 6 feet thick at base, are more frequently required.

MAGAZINES.

The simplest form of Magazine is that made by stout timbers from 10 feet to 12 feet in length, and 8 or 9 inches thick; placed against the flanks of the battery, or the least exposed part, at an angle of 45°; covered with a tarpaulin, and then with earth, or two or three rows of sand-bags.

N.B.—1. Although Gabion and Fascine revetments have been purposely omitted, as not being generally available to Seamen, a few remarks concerning them may prove useful.

Gabions are *cylindrical baskets*, open at both ends, usually about 3 feet in height, and 2 feet in diameter. They are placed on the parapet at the required slope, and being filled with earth from it, form an excellent support.

Fascines are *faggots* of superior construction. They are made of three lengths, 6, 12, and 18 feet, and are laid in the parapet in courses, each course occupying about 9 inches in height (the usual diameter of a fascine); and are secured by pickets driven through them into the parapet at intervals of 3 to 4 feet.

N.B.—2. It would be difficult to lay down any rules for ascertaining the time required to build a Redoubt or Battery, as that must entirely depend upon its extent, the consequent amount of excavation, the nature of the soil, and more particularly the number of available workmen; but some estimate may be formed, by stating that it has been found that an average workman can excavate from 6 *to* 8 *cubic feet* in a day of 8 *hours* under ordinary circumstances.

NOTE.—To be enabled to apply the foregoing rules, the Officer in charge of the working party must be acquainted with the names of the different parts of a Parapet and Ditch, and some of the principal technical terms in Field Fortification.